THE CONQUEST ON TRIAL

THE CONQUEST ON TRIAL

Carvajal's *Complaint of the Indians in the Court of Death*

Carlos A. Jáuregui

Introduction and Notes to
Michael de Carvajal's *Complaint of the Indians in the Court of Death* (1557)
by Carlos A. Jáuregui
Translation by Carlos A. Jáuregui and Mark Smith-Soto

The Pennsylvania State University Press
University Park, Pennsylvania

Library of Congress Cataloging-in-Publication Data

Carvajal, Micael de, ca. 1501-ca. 1576.
[Querella de los indios en Las cortes de la muerte. English]
The Conquest on trial : Carvajal's complaint of the indians in the court of death /
introduction and notes to Michael de Carvajal's complaint of the Indians in the
Court of Death (1557) by Carlos A. Jáuregui ; translation by Carlos A. Jáuregui
and Mark Smith-Soto.
         p.   cm.—(Latin American originals series)
Summary: "The first English translation of Michael de Carvajal's Spanish play
Complaint of the Indians in the Court of Death, originally published in 1557.
Translated by Carlos Jáuregui and Mark Smith-Soto. An annotated bilingual edition,
with an introduction that discusses the origins and ideological significance of the
play"—Provided by publisher.
Includes bibliographical references and index.
ISBN 978-0-271-02513-1 (pbk. : alk. paper)
1. Carvajal, Micael de, ca. 1501–ca. 1576. Querella de los indios en
Las cortes de la muerte.
2. America—Discovery and exploration—Spanish—Drama.
3. Indians, Treatment of—History—16th century—Drama.
I. Jáuregui, Carlos A.
II. Smith-Soto, Mark I. (Mark Israel), 1948– .
III. Title.

PQ6321.C35Q4713 2008
862'.3—dc22
2008013620

Copyright © 2008
The Pennsylvania State University
All rights reserved
Printed in the United States of America
Published by The Pennsylvania State University Press,
University Park, PA 16802-1003

The Pennsylvania State University Press is a member of the
Association of American University Presses.

It is the policy of The Pennsylvania State University Press to use acid-free paper.
This book is printed on Natures Natural, containing 50% post-consumer waste, and
meets the minimum requirements of American National Standard for Information
Sciences—Permanence of Paper for Printed Library Material, ANSI Z39.48–1992.

To Felipe, whose smile restores hope

CONTENTS

The Conquest on Trial, the third volume in the Latin American Originals (LAO) series, completes our inaugural trio of new perspectives on the Spanish conquests in the Americas. LAO 1, *Invading Colombia*, challenges us to view the disastrous Spanish invasion of Colombia in the 1530s as more representative of conquest campaigns than the better-known assaults on the Mexica and Inca empires. LAO 2, *Invading Guatemala*, shows how reading multiple accounts of conquest wars (in this case, Spanish, Nahua, and Maya versions of the Guatemalan conflict of the 1520s) can explode established narratives and suggest a conquest story that is more complicated, disturbing, and illuminating. LAO 3 continues in a similar vein. The book offers us an embassy of native Americans, filing a complaint over the conquest in a court in Spain—the Court of Death. The volume not only puts the Spanish conquest on trial for modern readers, but reveals how profound, complex, and (unfortunately) eternally relevant is the mid-sixteenth century debate over the Spanish invasions in the New World. Bartolomé de Las Casas was not the only Spaniard to question the motives and methods of the conquistadors; this play by Michael de Carvajal was the first theatrical examination of the conquest published in Spain, and it effectively condensed contemporary debates on conquest and colonization into one dramatic package.

The LAO series presents accessible, affordable editions of texts translated into English—often for the very first time. Some of the source texts were published in the colonial period in their original language (Spanish, Portuguese, or Latin), while others are archival documents written in Spanish or Portuguese or in indigenous languages such as Nahuatl, Zapotec, and Maya. The contributing authors are historians, anthropologists, art historians, and scholars of literature; they have developed a specialized knowledge that allows them to locate, translate, and present these texts in a way that contributes to scholars' understanding of the period, while also making them readable for students and nonspecialists.

Carlos A. Jáuregui is such an author. He teaches at Vanderbilt University as an associate professor of Latin American Literature and Anthropology; among his many writings on Latin American cultural history and literary expression is an award-winning book on cannibalism as a cultural metaphor. The world's leading scholar of Carvajal's play, Jáuregui published it in Spanish in Mexico in 2002; he has now collaborated with Mark Smith-Soto—a widely published and award-winning poet who teaches at the University of North Carolina, Greensboro, as a professor of Romance Languages—to produce the first English translation of this play ever to be printed. This edition is definitive; it includes a facsimile of the original play, a transcription of the Spanish text, an erudite introduction, and detailed notes. Presented thus, this brief but provocative piece of theatre is surely destined to be a classic.

—Matthew Restall

ACKNOWLEDGMENTS

Research for this book was possible thanks to the generous support of the Robert Penn Warren Center for the Humanities, the Program for Cultural Cooperation from Spain's Ministry of Education, the Instituto de Investigaciones Bibliográficas at the Universidad Nacional Autónoma de México (UNAM), and the Center for Latin American and Iberian Studies at Vanderbilt University. I gratefully acknowledge too the invaluable cooperation of the Biblioteca Nacional de España and the Biblioteca Nacional de México. I am especially indebted to the exceptional scholar and poet and dear friend Mark Smith-Soto, co-translator with me of Carvajal's *Complaint of the Indians in the Court of Death*, to the talented scholar and translator Juliet Lynd for her intelligent reading of the manuscript and her suggestions, and to my brilliant critic Joshua Lund for his comments. I also wish to thank the colleagues and friends who in many ways contributed to this book in different stages of its preparation, among them: Rolena Adorno, Beatriz de Alba-Koch, María Dolores Bravo, Vicky Burrus, José Pascual Buxó, Susan Castillo, Juan José Daneri, Edward F. Fischer, Edward H. Friedman, Dalia Hernandez, Cathy L. Jrade, Leah Marcus, Joseph S. Mella, John Morris, Alejandro Ortiz Bullé, Vicente Pérez de León, Phil Rasico, Matthew Restall, Juana Suarez, and David Patrick Wiseman.

Introduction: The Conquest on Trial

Carvajal's *Complaint of the Indians in the Court of Death*

CARLOS A. JÁUREGUI

[E]ven the dead will not be safe from the enemy if he wins.
And this enemy has not ceased to be victorious.
—Walter Benjamin

In Michael de Carvajal's *Complaint of the Indians in the Court of
Death*, a group of Indians and their chiefs, already converted to
Christianity, travels from the New World to Europe. There, before
a tribunal presided over by Death, they denounce the horrors and
crimes committed against them by the conquistadors and colonizers
in their idolatrous greed for gold. They ask either that the court take
away the power of these evil beings or that Death have mercy on
them and end their lives to put them out of their misery. Death recognizes the truth of what they say but asks them to have faith that
there will be divine justice in the end. Then Saint Augustine, Saint
Francis, and Saint Dominic, representing the three mendicant orders
evangelizing in the New World, ask the Indians to keep working
and trust in God. Saint Dominic even blames the Indies for having
corrupted Europe with so much wealth. Finally, Satan, Flesh, and
World intervene and explain, with cynical realism and not without
a certain sense of humor, that the reasons for the conquest are economic, ultimately having nothing to do with the project of evangelical salvation and everything to do with the gospel of desire (desire
for gold, for wealth, for indigenous labor, for pleasure). Thus, the
play ends without resolving the petition of the Indians, putting justice off until the afterlife and offering an unapologetic economic and
libidinal justification of colonialism (see below, Section 5).

Carvajal's *Complaint of the Indians* is a fundamental source
for the study of Latin American cultural history. One of the rare
sixteenth-century theatrical pieces about the Conquest of the New
World, perhaps the first one published in Spain,[1] it represents a condensed compendium of the debates of the day about the justification
of conquest, the right to wage war against the Indians, the evangelization of the natives, the discrimination against the newly converted
in the New World, the exploitation of Indian labor, the extent of the
emperor's sovereignty, and the right to resist tyranny. Furthermore,
Carvajal's work engages Bartolomé de Las Casas's theo-political
thought, employing many of his evangelical and political metaphors
and staging his ideas on war and colonization (see below, Section 4).
Yet, at the same time, it defuses and betrays the ultimate purpose
of Lascasian discourse (Section 5). This annotated, bilingual edition
offers the first English translation of this magnificent play as well as
a discussion of its origins and significance.

Descriptively titled here *Complaint of the Indians in the Court
of Death,* in Spanish the work is simply "Cena XIX" (Scene XIX)
of twenty-three dramatic pieces brought together under the title
*The Court of Death, to Which All Estates Come and by Means of
Representatives Warn the Living and Teach the Audience, in an
Elegant and Delicate Style. Addressed by Luis Hurtado de Toledo
to the Invincible Lord, Don Felipe, King of Spain and England, etc.,
Their Lord and King. In the Year of MDLvij*[2] (hereafter *The Court
of Death*). This moral dramatic work by Michael de Carvajal was
published by Luis Hurtado de Toledo (ca. 1523–90), with a few of his
own additions, on October 15, 1557, as part of a curious volume titled

---

1. Carvajal's *Complaint of the Indians in the Court of Death* is the first known
published Spanish play about the conquest of America (which is its central theme).
However, Indian characters and topics were already present in earlier plays, allegorical floats, and theatrical performances both in Spain and the New World; the theater
of evangelization also integrated native cultural elements into theatrical texts and
included an important presence of Indian actors in the production of the works. See
Consuelo Varela, "Las Cortes de la Muerte, ¿primera representación del indígena
americano en el teatro español?" in *Humanismo y tradición clásica en España y
América II,* ed. Jesús María Nieto Ibáñez (León, Spain: Universidad de León, Secretariado de Publicaciones, 2004), 343–44.

2. *Cortes de la Muerte a las cuales vienen todos los Estados, y por vía de representación, dan aviso a los vivientes y doctrina a los oyentes. Llevan gracioso y
delicado estilo. Dirigidas por Luis Hurtado de Toledo al invictísimo señor Don Felipe,
Rey de España y Inglaterra, etc., su señor y Rey. Año de MDLvij.*

The Court of Chaste Love and *The Court of Death*,[3] which brings various works on the theme of courtly love together with Carvajal's piece. *Complaint of the Indians* is not an "escena" (scene) in the sense of being one subdivision of an act in a play; rather, the scenes of *The Court of Death*, while thematically interrelated and sharing a similar structure, are relatively autonomous dramatic vignettes.

In these different scenes, various groups of allegorical or moral characters, representing the different estates of the kingdom[4] as well as different professions and nations, parade before Death. As universal judge, Death attends to their complaints of the injustices they have suffered and hears various petitions, including requests to postpone the final hour or to be given a liberating and merciful end. The characters are heterogeneous: shepherds, knights, rich men, prelates, a judge, frivolous nuns, philosophers, bandits, and so on. This macabre procession also includes a variety of other characters: Martin Luther (Hell's secretary), a group of Spanish Jews in exile, two Moors, and various American Indians and chieftains who lament their mistreatment and the cruelties committed against them in the New World. The cast of each piece includes a group of saints (Saint Augustine, Saint Jerome, Saint Francis, and Saint Dominic) that intervenes, as well as the opposing characters of Flesh, World, and Satan. Death, helped by the saints, lectures the complainants, asks them to reject the pleasures and possessions of the material world, and announces the final and definitive justice of God.

Given the number of scenes and their relative autonomy, it is possible that, as Joseph Gillet believes, *The Court of Death* was never staged, at least as a dramatic unit.[5] On the other hand, William Shoemaker maintains, looking at other multiple-scene plays from the period, that the length of *The Court of Death* is not per se an argument against the possibility of its being performed.[6] In fact,

3. *Cortes de casto amor y Cortes de la Muerte con algunas obras en metro y prosa de las que compuso, por él dirigidas al muy poderoso y muy alto señor Don Felipe, Rey de España y Inglaterra etc., su señor y Rey. Años 1557.*

4. That is, the clergy, the noblemen, and the commoners. See notes 3 and 4 to the play.

5. Joseph Gillet, introduction to *Tragedia Josephina*, by Michael de Carvajal, ed. Joseph Gillet (Princeton: Princeton University Press; Paris: Les Presses universitaires de France, 1932), lvi.

6. William Shoemaker, *The Multiple Stage in Spain During the Fifteenth and Sixteenth Centuries* (Princeton: Princeton University Press, 1935), 93.

frequent dramatic directions within the text—such as "The trumpets sound and the Indians enter" in *Complaint of the Indians*—would indicate that it was written to be performed. Furthermore, the structure of "retablos" or theatrical vignettes could even have facilitated the representation of one or a group of the different "escenas."

In general, information about sixteenth-century theatrical representations is scarce. The fact that we have two references to the staging of a play titled *Cortes de la Muerte* is remarkable: in 1571, the "tailor Diego de Berrío, resident of San Marcos, represented the play *El convite de Abraham*, winning one of the awards; the other one was given to Luis de Cerdeño [or Cerdeña] for the theatrical representation of *Las cortes de la Muerte*."[7] Sánchez Arjona believes that this may be "the same play represented the year before in that city by Cristóbal Hernández, and maybe that one published in 1557, started by Miguel de Carvajal, and finished by Luis Hurtado de Toledo."[8]

1. After the Dance, Death Goes to Court

The Court of Death is a moral, highly allegorical court drama whose theme, characters, and structure locate it within the tradition of the Dance of Death. Also known as "Danza de la Muerte," "Totentanz," "Danza macabra," or "Danse macabre," the Dance of Death is depicted on a vast array of paintings, engravings, and sculpted figures in which Death, as a dancing skeleton or as a corpse, appears to people from all different social positions and leads them in a dance or procession to the grave. While Death is normally personified as

---

7. José Sánchez Arjona, *Noticias referentes a los anales del teatro en Sevilla desde Lope de Rueda hasta fines del siglo XVII* (Seville: E. Rasco, 1898), 44; see also Miguel M. García-Bermejo Giner, *Catálogo del teatro español del siglo XVI: Índice de piezas conservadas, perdidas y representadas* (Salamanca: Ediciones Universidad de Salamanca, 1996), 239–41.

8. Sánchez Arjona, *Noticias referentes,* 44. Chapter 11 of the second part of *Don Quijote de la Mancha* (1615) concerns "the strange adventure that happened to the brave Don Quixote with the theatrical float *Las Cortes de la Muerte.*" Quixote encounters a group of actors from the Angulo el Malo company dressed for the play; however, as the list of characters given by Cervantes indicates, this is not Carvajal's piece, but rather Lope de Vega's *Las cortes de la Muerte.* See Carlos Jáuregui, *Querella de los indios en las Cortes de la Muerte (1557) de Michael de Carvajal* (Mexico City: Universidad Nacional Autónoma de México, 2002), 28–33.

a character, the living represent diverse groups, all confronting the equalizing impartiality of Death. This cultural tradition, which also includes literary, choreographic, and theatrical representations of allegorical, moral, or satirical characters in "a procession or dance, in which the living and the dead take a part," flourished toward the end of the Middle Ages and the beginning of the Renaissance (although it has roots in texts and motifs from classical Mediterranean antiquity).[9] It was connected to popular cultural anxieties about plagues, hunger, and war. Frequent and catastrophic epidemics during the fourteenth and fifteenth centuries, such as the Black Plague (1347–51), which killed nearly half of the population of Western Europe, and the Great Famine of Northern Europe (1315–22), presented people daily with the dreadful spectacle of the dead and the immediate possibility of dying. The world was often seen as a morbid scenario in which the ultimate result was the triumph of Death. All of this was reflected in popular culture, literature, and the arts through appalling depictions of suffering and carnage, as well as eschatological motifs, such as the symbolic use of the skeleton and the skull. The native populations of the New World also suffered such catastrophes; not long before the publication of *The Court of Death*, one of the worst plagues in human history killed 80 percent of the population of Mexico.[10] These plagues and catastrophes are echoed in *The Court of Death*, where the Indian characters constantly use pestilence and sickness as tropes. For them, the pestilence that brings death and destruction to the New World is colonial greed (see lines 43, 46, 86, 141, 191, 347).

One of the characteristics of the Dance of Death is the "arrangement of characters by estate; carefully graduated in rank they are passed in review, each one with an appropriate vice."[11] The Dance of

9. James Midgley Clark, *The Dance of Death in the Middle Ages and the Renaissance* (Glasgow: Jackson, 1950), 1–2.

10. The epidemic of *cocoliztli* (Nahuatl for "pest") of 1545–48 "killed an estimated 5 million to 15 million people, or up to 80% of the native population of Mexico. In absolute and relative terms the 1545 epidemic was one of the worst demographic catastrophes in human history, approaching even the Black Death of bubonic plague, which killed approximately 25 million in Western Europe from 1347 to 1351 or about 50% of the regional population." Rodolfo Acuña-Soto, David W. Stahle, Malcolm K. Cleaveland, and Matthew D. Therrell, "Megadrought and Megadeath in 16th Century Mexico," *Historical Review* 8 (2002): 360.

11. Florence Whyte, *The Dance of Death in Spain and Catalonia* (Baltimore: Waverly Press, 1931), vii–viii.

Death not only called men to a realization of mortality (*memento mori*), it also alleviated such a fate through an equalizing and sometimes festive or carnivalistic representation of Death. After all, there is some relief in seeing kings, cardinals, noblemen, tax collectors, lawyers, and the pope share the same fate as paupers and peasants; before Death, everybody is naked of privilege and distinction and appears as a human sinner waiting for decay and judgment; ready to dance with Death, so to speak.[12] The Dance of Death presented a procession of all humanity to the grave, with Death often admonishing each mortal. Textual, musical, and sometimes performative, the Dance was a cautionary representation of mortality with the implicit or explicit invitation to all men and women to repent and prepare themselves to better await their ultimate fate. This is the invitation to the different estates found in the song-poem "Ad mortem festinamus" from the *Llibre Vermell* (ca. 1399), preserved in the abbey of Montserrat, near Barcelona: "Ad mortem festinamus peccare desistamus" (We hurry toward death, let us desist from sin). Among the numerous examples of Dances of Death,[13] the most representative Dance in Spanish is the anonymous *Dança general [de la Muerte]*. Written around the second half of the fourteenth century, it is part of a codex in the library of the Escorial.[14] As in *The Court of Death*, in the *Dança general* Death summons the mortals, listens to them (mostly their complaints of having to die), and censures their sins and their vanity or simply states their final destiny. For example, Death tells the emperor that he will not be saved by the empire, nor

---

12. The Dance of Death does not necessarily imply dancing; dancing, like eating and loving, symbolizes life, and like life itself, is ultimately a movement toward death and the sepulcher.

13. These include *Dança general de la Muerte* (ca. 1390–1400), *Joch o el entremés de la Mort* (1412), *La dança general de la muerte* (1520), and the *Dança de la morte: E de aquelles persones qui mal llur grat ab quella ballen e dançen* (ca. 1497). The last is a translation into Catalan of the French *Danse macabre* (1485), transcribed by Pere Miquel Carbonell. Other works within this tradition include the trilogy *Auto de barca do inferno* (1517), *Auto da barca do purgatorio* (1518), and *Auto de la barca de la gloria* (1519) by Gil Vicente, as well as *Farsa llamada Dança dela Muerte* (1551) by Joan de Pedraza. For more on the Dance of Death, see the wide array of works discussing such diverse aspects of the genre as its graphic and literary representations, its roots in popular medieval culture, and its festive aspects (e.g., Florence Whyte, Joël Saugnieux, Fritz Eichenberg, Jurgis Baltrusaitis, Guglielmo Invernizzi, Nicoletta Della Casa and Maria Canella, and Víctor Infantes).

14. Manuscrito b.IV.21, Biblioteca del Monasterio del Escorial.

by his "gold, silver, and other metals," because—says Death—"here is where you lose all your possessions / and all you have acquired with great tyranny / by waging never-ending wars."[15] In Carvajal's play, the Indians make similar calculations, but for the conquistadors (151–60). The *Dança general* has many other points of contact with *The Court of Death,* such as the leading character, the parade of different estates (who are lectured by Death about their sins and their vanity), and, to a certain extent, the organization of the text as a series of speeches by Death and the mortal characters. The scenario, however, is different: a series of appearances in court (*Cortes*) replaces the parade or dance of mortals before Death. The Spanish word "Cortes" in the play can refer to two different things: a tribunal or judge that hears and resolves cases, or the advisory council or representative assembly of the estates of the kingdom—nobility, clergy, towns (the people or commoners)—reunited by royal convocation to decide important political issues.[16]

The Court of Death certainly constitutes a dramatic reelaboration of the Dance of Death, theatrically staging the main elements of the Dance. However, while *The Court of Death* cites and uses the premodern model of the Dance, it barely hides an undeniable political modernity, in two senses. First, it conceptualizes the empire as a sovereign power that observes and manages multiplicity and difference. Second, we find in it the emergent anxieties and conflicts associated with the expansion of that sovereign power, that is, the strife brought about by religious absolutism, imperialism, and colonization. Scene III, for instance, is a Counter-Reformationist condemnation of Lutheranism and other Protestant "sects." Luther "the traitor," dead since 1546, appears as the secretary of Satan; he is the "source of heresies" and an "attorney / for the lawsuits of Hell," and Satan and his friends let the audience know that "Mohammed and the like"—English Protestants and other heretics—already have a special seat reserved for them in Hell, where "they will be turned into charcoal."[17] The Counter-Reformationism of Carvajal's play goes along with its patent Erasmism. Since the 1530s, Erasmus's influence had been repressed due to suspicions of sympathy with

15. "Aquí perderedes el vuestro cabdal / que atesorastes con grand tiranía, / façendo batallas de noche e de día." *Dança general,* 32, lines 113–20.

16. See note 4 to the play.

17. Fol. 7r.

illuminist heterodoxies and Lutheranism and to its moral critique of ecclesiastic authorities. In an Erasmist way, *The Court of Death* discusses and censures the morals and religiosity of ambitious and dissolute bishops and clerics (Scene IV) as well as disobedient and worldly nuns (Scene X). Other examples of Erasmism can be found in Scene VI, a condemnation of war (except against the heretics),[18] a matter that will also appear prominently in the *Complaint of the Indians*. So while *The Court of Death* resembles the Dance of Death, it includes scenes in which several modern conflicts related to the empire are vented before the universal, indeed, higher sovereignty of Death.

Sufficient attention has not yet been paid to this remarkable dramatic work, despite the fact that it constitutes a true sound box in which one can hear the political and religious tensions of the empire in Europe and in America (as well as their dogmatic resolutions).[19] In addition to the conflicts of the Counter-Reformation and the sermons of the Erasmist cause, the play also engages the debate surrounding the mendicant orders and Cardinal Cisneros's reforms (Scene VIII), peasant struggles for land (Scene XVI), the

18. The characters who participate in Scene VI are Knight, Death, Saint Augustine, Saint Jerome, and Satan. The knight comes to solicit "on behalf of a thousand lords / on behalf of kings and emperors / and the military State" as well as "dukes, counts, [and] marquises" (fol. 13v). He demands longevity for those whom he represents and implores Death not to "take them with you as you are accustomed to, /. . . / because they are now occupied / with great, cruel wars" and because they have not had time to repent; so if the scythe of death cuts them down, they will go directly to Hell (fol. 13v). Death (now following Erasmus) asks them to stop the wars and to struggle "against the world and its vices"; Saint Augustine asks them to be the "Christian cavalry" and to wage "wars / against the Devil" (fol. 14r); Saint Jerome invites them to hold the cross as their only weapon (fol. 14v); and Death now requires that they direct their wars against the "sects" of heretics. Satan concludes by commenting that Hell has more military men than any other group of sinners (fol. 15r).

19. There are, of course, exceptions to this general indifference by critics. The most enlightening discussions of Scene XIX are Juan Ortega y Medina, "El indio absuelto y las Indias condenadas en las *Cortes de la muerte*," *Historia Mexicana* 4 (1954–55): 477–505; Francisco Ruiz Ramón, *América en el teatro clásico español: Estudio y textos* (Pamplona: Ediciones Universidad de Navarra, 1993), 19–25; and Susan Castillo, *Performing America: Colonial Encounters in New World Writing, 1500–1786* (London: Routledge, 2005), 83–88. Valentín Pedro devotes a chapter to Scene XIX: Pedro, *América en las letras españolas del Siglo de Oro* (Buenos Aires: Editorial sudamericana, 1954), 45–65. One must also note studies such as that of Fe María de Varona Finch, which offers a very good general presentation of the entire work: Finch, "A Study of *Las Cortes de la Muerte* by Micael de Carvajal and Luis Hurtado de Toledo" (M.A. thesis, University of North Carolina at Chapel Hill, 1982).

renewed challenges to nobility rights, and—in the case that occupies us here—the burning question of the justification of the overseas Empire and the domination of the New World. In effect, Carvajal's *Complaint of the Indians in the Court of Death* constitutes a dramatic allegorical *summa* of the modern formation of imperial reason (the political, legal, and theological justification of the empire) and of the moral doubts and debates with respect to the Conquest of the New World and the domination of the Indians (see below, Sections 3–5).

2. Elusive Author(s): Michael de Carvajal and Luis Hurtado de Toledo

The authorship of *The Court of Death* is not clear, to say the least. According to Luis Hurtado de Toledo, who published it, the work "was begun by Michael de Carvajal, native of Plasencia, and I, in admiration of its style, did continue and complete it." That, at least, is what he says in his dedicatory to Philip II. Little is known, however, about Michael de Carvajal, despite the relative fame of his *Tragedia Josefina* (1535).[20] There are two known contemporaneous persons who might have written *The Court of Death*, both named Miguel de Carvajal and both from Plasencia, a city in the province of Cáceres, in the region of Extremadura in western Spain.[21] The author could be the buoyant and insolvent Miguel de Carvajal (1500?–ca. 1575), who lived in economic hardship and was hounded by judicial matters. But the play could also have been written by the other Miguel de Carvajal, born between 1490 and 1510, the fortunate heir of a family of means, who is known to have been in Santo Domingo in 1534. Or, for all we know, it could have been written by

20. *Tragedia Josephina* (Joseph's Tragedy) (1535?, 1540, 1545, 1546) was impeccably edited and studied by Joseph Gillet. The play's central story is that of the biblical patriarch Joseph, represented as a prefiguration of Christ. His own invidious and jealous brothers, jealous that their father favors Joseph, conspire to sell him as a slave to a group of merchants, who in turn sell him to Potiphar, officer of Pharaoh. Joseph gets in trouble thanks to Potiphar's wife Zenobia, who calumniates him after he refuses her amorous requests. Joseph's visionary abilities save him as he interprets Pharaoh's dreams and becomes his advisor and protégé. Finally, Joseph faces his brothers and pardons them.

21. This same region was the native home of many of the conquistadors of America, including Hernán Cortés, the Pizarros, and Pedro de Valdivia.

a third Miguel or Michael de Carvajal of Plasencia who is otherwise unknown to us.

The Insolvent Carvajal

The life of the first Miguel de Carvajal remains a mystery; even the most basic biographical data such as date of birth and death, details about his education, and his occupation other than letters are unclear. Most information comes from legal and court documents,[22] a circumstance that makes Carvajal's life look like a series of economic difficulties and conflicts with his close relatives, his creditors, and his wife.

Miguel was the son of Hernando de Carvajal and Isabel Almaraz. In 1534, he married Teresa Núñez de Almaraz, with whom he had a legitimate daughter, Rufina, who became a nun in the Convent of Santa Clara, Plasencia.[23] Based on the date of his marriage, we conjecture that he was born between 1500 and 1515. He was initially a well-off man who irresponsibly borrowed and wasted all of his money and the money of others[24] and drove himself to insolvency. His mother often had to foot the bill to get him out of financial troubles; even in her will (1557), she expressed an evident lack of confidence in him.[25] A master of spending beyond his means, he

22. These documents include the testament of Isabel Almaraz, Miguel's mother, in which he appears as a spendthrift son (August 31, 1557); a legal claim against him by Teresa Núñez, his wife, asking for the refund of her dowry and legal protection against Miguel's creditors (November 9, 1556); a deed by which Miguel, on his deathbed, refunded the dowry (August 31, 1575); the testament of the nun Rufina de Carvajal, his daughter (November 1556); and a contract between his wife Teresa (by then a widow) and her brother (1578). These documents were uncovered more than a century ago by Vicente Paredes and are quoted here from his transcription.

23. This information comes from the testament of Isabel Almaraz and the testament of Rufina de Carvajal, which is partially transcribed by Paredes. See Vicente Paredes, "Micael de Carvajal, el trágico," *Revista de Extremadura* 1 (1899): 366–72. Apparently, Carvajal had more children (illegitimate), who are mentioned in passing in his mother's testament.

24. In 1542, he tried to get money from his brother-in-law, a minor, persuading him to sell a rental from lands inherited from an aunt (ibid., 367).

25. In the event that Miguel and Teresa Núñez split up, Miguel's mother arranged to have her granddaughter Rufina's inheritance managed by her sons-in-law, not by Miguel. Moreover, foreseeing her son's imminent and complete ruin, she authorized the sale of any property or rent necessary to attend to Miguel's basic needs, on the condition that the money be given to him "little by little" (ibid., 368). Miguel did not divorce Teresa Núñez, but apparently he never changed his ways.

sought his father's estate (to his mother's dismay),[26] and later, his wife's dowry. A year before the publication of *The Court of Death*, Teresa Núñez tried to save her patrimony from her husband's mismanagement by asking a magistrate for an order for the devolution of her dowry so as to separate it from her husband's patrimony (November 1556).[27] According to Teresa, her husband had mortgaged his and her properties, was broke, and had fled his creditors.[28] Almost twenty years later, on his deathbed, Miguel finally signed the papers separating the dowry from his patrimony (1575); or rather, a witness had to sign for him, since Miguel was too sick. Maybe there were still creditors after him, but in any case, he died soon thereafter.[29]

Although Paredes and Gillet claim that this Miguel is the one who wrote the *Tragedia Josephina* and *The Court of Death*, none of the information obtained from these documents makes it possible to confirm this. His name appears once in a legal document as "Micael," which is close to the spelling "Michael" in the published plays.[30] Two

26. His father died in 1548, and soon thereafter Miguel asked his mother for his share of his father's estate. She was at odds with him for his "disobedient and mischievous behavior" and perhaps for claiming his inheritance to dissipate it, as he did with every penny he put his hands on. Isabel Almaraz deducted Miguel's inheritance from her gifts, and she even overvalued some of the goods given to him. His mother recounts how Miguel accepted her accounting, stating that "as an obedient son he did not want to fight with me in court" (ibid., 369).

27. She states, "The aforesaid husband of mine has plunged into poverty and diminished the patrimony with his mismanagement, he has skipped town because of some debts, and he has sold his assets and mine, or at least most of them, and that is why I need, why I am indeed forced to reclaim my dowry and properties" (ibid., 368).

28. Although she was suing Miguel, she was actually defending her interests from her husband's creditors, who were trying to take her dowry along with the rest of Miguel's properties that they could seize and sell off.

29. "The aforementioned Miguel de Carvajal . . . expressed that he was not able to sign for himself because his hand was unresponsive, so he asked Juan de Borgoñon, a witness, to sign for him" (Paredes, "Micael de Carvajal, el trágico," 370). Teresa already had the possession of those properties, so the deed was a mere formality to legalize the ownership titles. In a document dated August 30, 1578, she signed as "widow of Miguel de Carvajal" (370–71).

30. Paredes notes that Rufina Carvajal's testament uses the Latin spelling ("Micael") of her father's name: "Last Will of Rufina de Carvajal, daughter of Micael de Carvajal and Tereza Núñez" (ibid., 372). That spelling also appears in both *Tragedia Josephina* (1535) and in *The Court of Death* with a small variation: "Michael." It is important to keep in mind that sometimes names such as Miguel were Hispanic versions of Latinized names given at birth, and Latinized spellings such as Michael or Micael were common for use in publications.

textual references in *The Court of Death* may also support the case for his authorship. First, in Scene X,[31] the nun who represents the estate comes from Spain and—just like the daughter of the insolvent Carvajal—belongs to the Order of Santa Clara.[32] Second, the clear antipathy toward judges and lawyers seen in Scenes XIII and XIV, although common in the tradition of the *Dance of Death*, is more consistent with somebody like the insolvent Carvajal than with the other, prosperous Carvajal, who benefited all of his life from litigation.

The Prosperous Carvajal

The second Miguel de Carvajal who may have written *The Court of Death*, Miguel de Carvajal Arlnate, also emerges in court documents related to a case handled by the magistrate of Plasencia and in an appeal by the *Cancillería* of Valladolid from 1548 to 1549.[33] Also born in Plasencia around 1490–1510, he was the illegitimate son of the wealthy Alonso de Carvajal, owner of many houses and vineyards, and Juana García, a single woman from Gargantaolalla who apparently disappeared from Miguel's life early on.[34] Don Alonso died unmarried in October of 1525 and left his "fortune, houses and vineyards . . . as well as the principal mill, an olive field and another vineyard" to his brother Álvaro de Carvajal, who was required to pay one-third of all the inheritance to his sister Teresa and another third to his other brother Hernando (last will of September 25, 1525). He also stipulated that Teresa had to leave her third to Miguel after her death.[35] Teresa was the most appropriate person to take care of Miguel, since she had in fact raised him. In her last will (February 12, 1548), she declared: "because I care for and love my nephew Miguel de Carvajal, whom I raised . . . I make him the only and universal heir to all of my belongings. . . . As for the real estate properties I have, which are not mine since I only

31. Fols. 254–31r.

32. Fol. 25r.

33. These documents are partially published in Narciso Alonso Cortés, "Miguel de Carvajal," *Hispanic Review* 2 (1933): 141–48, and will be cited to that work.

34. One witness says that Miguel was known in the city as the son of Alonso de Carvajal, and that as for his mother, Juana García, "he [the witness] said that he did not remember her" (ibid., 143).

35. Ibid., 142–44.

have lifetime rights of usufruct, they belong to Miguel de Carvajal."[36] Miguel's uncles later contributed to his good fortune: Hernando de Carvajal, who lived in Santo Domingo during the 1530s, had designated his brother Álvaro as *patrono* (executive) of a *capellanía*, a lucrative fund with pious objectives.[37] Álvaro died in July of 1530 without accepting the capellanía, so Hernando instituted a new capellanía in 1534 and designated his nephew Miguel as its *patrono*, effectively giving him control of the funds and properties donated and all of their profits (after providing for the satisfaction of the pious obligations). The sons of the late Álvaro de Carvajal disputed Miguel's rights and pretended that the first capellanía in favor of their father was irrevocable and had preeminence over the second of 1534. Miguel successfully alleged in court that the first donation was incomplete because it had not been accepted. The Carvajal cousins lost the case (June 5, 1544), appealed, and lost again.[38] In the middle of the appeal, Teresa died, leaving her nephew Miguel all of her possessions.[39]

One of the most notable facts emerging from these court documents is that by 1534, Carvajal was in the New World, in Santo Domingo. During the litigation in 1544, a witness states that Miguel traveled to Santo Domingo to accept the donation: "the said Miguel de Carvajal, son of the aforementioned bachelor Alonso de Carvajal, went to the Indies where the said Hernando de Carvajal, his uncle, lived and had his home, and where he made that donation to his nephew."[40] Thus, Miguel de Carvajal would have visited the

---

36. Ibid., 147–48.

37. A capellanía is a donation that came with certain obligations, such as paying for masses for the soul of the benefactor (*fundador*) or fulfilling other pious obligations defined by him or her. See Martín Alonso Pedraz, *Diccionario medieval español: Desde las Glosas emilianenses y silenses (s.X) hasta el siglo XV* (Salamanca: Universidad Pontificia de Salamanca, 1986), s.v. "capellanía."

38. *Cancillería* of Valladolid, August 7, 1549.

39. Cortés, "Miguel de Carvajal," 147–48.

40. Cortés, "Miguel de Carvajal," 146. This fact was noted by Cortés (ibid.) and later commented on by Pedro Henríquez Ureña: "Micael or Miguel de Carvajal was in Santo Domingo in 1534. By then, he had written already, or would have been writing *Tragedia Josephina*, printed in 1535, and one of the masterpieces of the Spanish theatre before Lope de Vega. He was . . . from Plasencia, where he was born around 1499; on October 14, 1534, his uncle Hernando de Carvajal gave him in Santo Domingo . . . the patronage of the *capellanía* he had instituted in 1528, for the Church of San Martín, in Plasencia." Pedro Henríquez Ureña, *La cultura y las letras coloniales en Santo Domingo* (Buenos Aires: Universidad de Buenos Aires, 1936), 57 n4. Consuelo Varela

Indies and had the opportunity to see firsthand the devastation of the indigenous population in Santo Domingo. He probably also knew about the conflicts between the Order of Saint Dominic and the *encomenderos* and the ill-treatment and forced labor imposed on the Indians, which is one of the main topics of *Complaint of the Indians*. More importantly, Carvajal would certainly have known about the insurrection of the Indian rebel Enriquillo and his guerrilla war (1519–33) against the *encomienda* and colonial rule, and about the negotiated end of the war with Enriquillo through the Paz de Barrionuevo treaty (August 4, 1533) and the persuasive intervention of Las Casas, who exhorted Enriquillo to remain faithful to the emperor after the treaty. Indian insurgence and colonial domination are key topics in *Complaint of the Indians* (see below, Section 5).

Did Carvajal meet Las Casas or other friars defending the Indians while in Santo Domingo?[41] While there, did he develop some sort of sympathy for the Indian cause after the Paz de Barrionuevo? If so, would such sympathy not have been in conflict with the economic interests of his uncle? Did he use his American experience to compose the play? We will probably never know for sure, but this Caribbean connection certainly weighs in favor of the prosperous Carvajal as the author of *The Court of Death*.

In a book of poems published in 1636, on the occasion of Lope de Vega's death, Fabio Franchi mentions "Miguel de Plasencia" as one of the "famous dramatists from the first epoch."[42] Famous as he may have been then, over time Michael de Carvajal faded away into a handful of textual fragments and incomplete pieces of legal disputes related to two different individuals between whom we cannot choose. Should we side with the dissipated Carvajal, surrounded by creditors, sued by his wife, and rescued time after time by his mother? Or that other Carvajal, the lucky illegitimate son of a rich man who

---

has not found Hernando de Carvajal among the lists of passengers to the Indies: Varela, "Las Cortes de la Muerte, ¿primera representación del indígena americano en el teatro español?" in *Humanismo y tradición clásica en España y América II*, ed. Jesús María Nieto Ibáñez (León, Spain: Universidad de León, Secretariado de Publicaciones, 2004), 338–39.

41. Carvajal was in Santo Domingo by October 1534, if not before. Las Casas's Carta al Consejo de Indias, written in Santo Domingo, was dated April 30, 1534.

42. Cayetano Alberto de la Barrera y Leirado, *Catálogo bibliográfico y biográfico del teatro antiguo español: Desde sus orígenes hasta mediados del Siglo XVIII* (Madrid: M. Rivadeneyra, 1860), 72.

was raised and pampered by his aunt and who traveled to America and inherited several fortunes? At this point it is impossible to know which of them (if it was either one) wrote *The Court of Death*.

Luis Hurtado de Toledo, Admirer, Editor, and (Maybe) Coauthor

Luis Hurtado de Toledo, publisher of *The Court of Death*, was the son of Juan Sánchez de San Pedro, from Murcia, and Leonor de la Fuente Hurtado. Although some critics believe that he was born around 1510,[43] Hurtado de Toledo himself, in testimony given in 1585 during the Inquisition trial of a painter, declared that he was sixty-eight years old, which means that he was born around 1523.[44] For most of his life he was the parish priest of the San Vicente de Toledo Chapel, where he died on March 15, 1590.[45] Apparently he enjoyed some prestige as a man of letters, since he was "appointed to write down the answers to a questionnaire sent by Philip II to the cities and villages in 1576, inquiring about the situation and needs of the kingdom."[46]

Hurtado de Toledo's "questionable publishing practices" have put him at the center of various controversies.[47] These practices included not identifying the author, placing his own name prominently on other authors' works that he published, and—in some cases—attributing someone else's work as his own.[48] As William

---

43. Antonio Rodríguez-Moñino, "El poeta Luis Hurtado de Toledo," in *Las Cortes de la Muerte*, by Luis Hurtado de Toledo and Michael Carvajal (Valencia: Librería Bonaire, 1964), 32–33.

44. Ángel Vegue y Goldoni established these dates based on the files of a case before the Inquisition of Toledo against the painter Francisco Becerra. See Vegue y Goldoni, "Apuntaciones para la biografía de Luis Hurtado de Toledo," in *Temas de arte y de literatura*, 58–59 (Madrid: Imprenta Iris, 1928). See also Finch, "A Study of *Las Cortes de la Muerte*," 9–12.

45. Antonio Blanco Sánchez, *Entre Fray Luis y Quevedo: En busca de Francisco de la Torre* (Salamanca: Gráficas Cervantes, 1982), 227–29. Hurtato de Toledo's death is recorded on the register of the deceased ("Libro de difuntos") of the parish, found by Vegue y Goldoni ("Apuntaciones para la biografía de Luis Hurtado de Toledo," 59).

46. Vegue y Goldoni, "Apuntaciones para la biografía de Luis Hurtado de Toledo," 57.

47. Finch, "A Study of *Las Cortes de la Muerte*," 12.

48. That is indeed what happened with two other works published together with *The Court of Death: Hospital for Ladies Wounded by Love, by One of the Same: Beautiful, Wise and Witty, Although for Those Reasons All the More Injured*

Purser said, "wherever Hurtado's name appears, something strange will probably also appear."[49] Hurtado de Toledo claims, in his dedication of *The Court of Death* to Philip II, to have finished the work: "it was begun by Michael de Carvajal, native of Plasencia, and I, in admiration of its style, did continue and complete it."[50] The consensus among critics regarding is that Carvajal wrote *The Court of Death* and Hurtado de Toledo, in publishing it, inserted some stanzas and lines here and there. Antonio Rodríguez-Moñino, for example, says that Hurtado de Toledo did practically nothing: "I think that *The Court of Death* is a work by Micael de Carvajal, composed by him alone, given its perfect stylistic harmony, the steady sharp way in which the play carries the action from beginning to end, and given the fast pace and ingenuity of the plot, without the mythological digressions that Luis Hurtado liked so much. Ultimately, it is Carvajal's work because every one of its lines is saying so. If Hurtado de Toledo put his quill in the text it must have been only for such minimal changes that they disappear within Carvajal's work."[51] Likewise, Gillet considers that Hurtado de Toledo "perhaps contributed the *Introito* (although it seems too well written to be his) and, more probably, the entrance of 'Vasco de Figueyra, a Portuguese Christian' (Scene XX), an incongruous character . . . because, unless the Portuguese must be considered as a special kind of Christian, his coming breaks up the series of representation types who appear in succession before the tribunal of Death."[52]

Hurtado de Toledo unquestionably made some changes in order to establish links between the works of the first part of the volume

---

and *Mirror of Courtesy for Ladies and Gentlemen by the Author from Toledo, Who Wrote the Hospitals of Love Mirror of Courtesy.* The latter, according to Rodríguez-Moñino, was a "cheap plagiarism and summary of *Doctrinal de gentileza* by Hernando de Ludueña, printed as early as 1514" ("El poeta Luis Hurtado de Toledo," 17).

49. In Finch, "A Study of *Las Cortes de la Muerte*," 14. Despite all these "questionable publishing practices," Hurtado de Toledo did write some pieces of his own, such as *Égloga Silviana del galardón de amor* (1553), *Cortes de casto amor* (1557), and *Trescientas de Luys Hurtado* (1582) (see ibid., and Rodríguez-Moñino, "El poeta Luis Hurtado de Toledo," 15, 39, 45, 46).

50. Fol. 2r.

51. Rodríguez-Moñino, "El poeta Luis Hurtado de Toledo," 19.

52. Gillet, introduction to *Tragedia Josephina*, xvi.

(devoted to courtly love) and Carvajal's *The Court of Death*.[53] Beyond this, detecting Hurtado de Toledo's involvement in the work becomes very problematic. One can always find rough lines here and there, structural inconsistencies, and dramatic irregularities that may be the work of Hurtado de Toledo;[54] but without Carvajal's manuscript it is practically impossible to say what Hurtado de Toledo's "continue and complete" actually mean.

There is no evidence that Carvajal complained about Hurtado's bold claim of coauthorship. Gillet offers two hypotheses to explain this: either Carvajal "in a medieval spirit of dedication *ad majorem dei gloriam*, disclaimed all sense of literary ownership" or "in the atmosphere of sharpened intolerance surrounding the accession of Philip II, the boldness of the social and religious criticism in the *Cortes* might well have made the author fear to tread where Hurtado, dedicating the work to the King himself, rushed in without misgiving."[55] Rodríguez-Puértolas speculates that Carvajal was dissuaded from suing Hurtado de Toledo by the Erasmism of the work, since "by 1557 and 1558 Spain was engaged in a violent persecution of Erasmism."[56] Was this play heterodox enough to make its author reticent to claim authorship? Long before Erasmus, the tradition of the Dance of Death conventionally included harsh criticisms of the corruption of the Church authorities, nuns, and kings. These moral reprimands were abstract enough not to displease the authorities. Philip II himself collected the *Dança general de la Muerte* for the library of the Escorial in 1576. By using and quoting the conventions of the Dance of Death within a Counter-Reformationist ideology (featuring attacks on Lutheranism and other "sects"), Carvajal concealed the more or less heterodox Erasmism of the play.

There are other possible explanations for Carvajal's silence. We know that the insolvent Carvajal was alive when the play was

---

53. At the end of Scene XXI, for example, there is a mention of Cupid and the Court of Love (fol. 64r); this is a reference to another work published in the same volume: *The Court of Chaste Love on the Flowering Bank of the Tajo River in the Royal Palaces of the Maritime Forest*. Also, in the first lines of the unusually short Scene XXII, the author, as a character, metafictionally participates in the court and refers to "that other Court of Love" (fol. 65r) and later, to Minerva and Cupid.

54. Finch makes a very thorough effort to find these possible interpolations ("A Study of *Las Cortes de la Muerte*," 106–16).

55. Gillet, introduction to *Tragedia Josephina*, xviii.

56. Rodríguez-Puértolas, 657.

published, so if he did not claim the authorship it could have been because he was not the author or did not know about the publication. On the other hand, the last news we have about the prosperous Carvajal is that in 1549 he won the case against his cousins. He may have not been alive in 1557, and therefore would obviously have been unable to challenge Hurtado de Toledo. We need also to consider that the idea that authors own their creations, as well as the modern notion of authorship itself, are historically and socially constructed. In the middle of the sixteenth century, authorship was not judicially recognized as a property right. In any case, Luis Hurtado de Toledo's importance does not lie in the truth of his alleged coauthorship of *The Court of Death*, but in the fact that by publishing it, he saved it from oblivion. Between the contemporaneous Carvajales from Plasencia and Hurtado de Toledo, a priest prone to publishing and enmeshing himself in the authorship of his editions, the matter of the author of *The Court of Death* remains indeterminable, a tailor-made case for the poststructuralist "death of the author."[57]

3. The Case in Question

Complaining Indians

Escena XIX begins with eleven interventions by various indigenous characters in the Court of Death, corresponding to the first 320 lines (about 71 percent of the piece).[58] In the initial presentation of the case (lines 1–120), the chieftain introduces the plaintiffs: several Indians and their chieftains who have come from the New World to air their grievances in court (1–10). Thanks to the royal sovereigns and evangelizers, they have already converted to Christianity, and so they do not understand why they are the victims of so many cruelties (11–25). When they were not Christians, says the chieftain, nobody bothered them, nor robbed them, nor waged war against them as they do now (26–50). Furthermore, the Indians want to know why, having their own responsibilities to their

---

57. I am referring to the classic essays by Roland Barthes, "La mort de l'auteur," and Michel Foucault, "Qu'est-ce qu'un auteur?"
58. See note 9 to the play.

families and dependents, they must also maintain and "enrich . . . all other human kind," including the English, the Hungarians, the Bohemians, the French, the Spaniards, and the Genoese (51–65). The chieftain fears that not even the New World with its many precious metals will be able to satisfy colonial desire, and he wonders if the reason these monstrous "giants" are devoting so much effort to plundering the riches of the Indies is that they have already exhausted the riches of the rest of the world (including Arabia, Sheba, Tharshish, and Narsinga). He declares that the Indians may have to flee their homeland to escape these brutal people and their evil hunger for gold (66–90) and explains that the Indians do not value gold, the price of which has proven to be the copious spilling of innocent blood and so much injustice and corruption. It is the Europeans' quest for gold, says the chieftain, that accounts for the death, mutilation, and slaughter suffered by the Indians (91–120).

A character designated "Other Indian" [Otro indio] follows the chieftain, insisting on the evangelical paradox: he does not understand how it can be that the Indians, who are good Christians, are treated like brutes. The Indians may be New Christians—"latecomers to the vineyards of the Lord"—but, as far as they understand from the lessons of Christianity preached in the Indies, God does not make distinctions between latecomers and the early birds (111–40).

At this point, the chieftain (it is not clear from the text if this is the same character who opened the scene or a different one) reminds the court of the case of the Roman general and triumvir Marcus Licinius Crassus, who, enriched by mining as well as the slave trade, was captured by the Parthians and forced to drink molten gold. The chieftain proposes that the same medicine be used to cure the colonial thirst for metals. He adds that the Indians have learned that not one of these ravenous men will be able to take any gold with him to the afterlife; rather, they will lose their souls because of it (141–65). Following this provocative suggestion, another Indian character, designated simply as "Another" (Otro), clearly denounces the hypocrisy of the evangelizing mission of the Indies. He insists that according to those teachings, God must "be loved above all" and that one must not harm one's neighbor. But, he points out, the hypocrites who exploit the Indies and the Indians distort everything: they advertise wine but are actually selling vinegar. He notes that it is hard to believe that the wrath of God does not punish such dreadful iniquities on the spot (166–80). A chieftain (probably another character) points out that, unlike the Indians, these men are idolaters whose love of gold would drive them to rob even Christ himself. This Indian proposes a solution distinct from the earlier suggestion that the conquistadors be forced to drink molten gold: the Indians must go into exile to escape the pestilence of gold wrought upon their lands (181–210). This same chieftain presents a humorous paradox: while Ptolemy and other cartographers were unable to find the New World, greed managed to locate the Indies with no trouble at all (211–40).

Another Indian then accuses the Europeans of bringing all the sins of the Old World to the Indies, and he declares that the Indians would rather see their children die than allow them to learn all these evils (241–50). He also voices a pacifist position censuring the wars and modern weapons (such as harquebuses and steel swords) used to spill human blood. He asks, not without irony, if the Indians are the warlike and violent ones (251–60). The chieftain confirms that the Indians are not the aggressors; he conjectures that it is precisely because the Indians are peaceful that they are attacked and robbed. He suggests that the Europeans try their hand with the pugnacious Amazons (261–70) instead of attacking quiet people who have done nothing to provoke war (271–80).

Another Indian professes his disdain for wealth and says that those who have that ill thirst for it can have it and poison themselves with their riches. The Indians, as the chieftain has already pointed out (91–97), do not care for gold; they are perfectly content with their sense of right and wrong. The Indians suppose that in this respect there might be a different understanding of Christian philosophy in Europe (281–300).

Finally, yet another Indian makes a concrete request of the court: to remove those ambitious tyrants from power, or, if that is not possible, to let the Indians receive a merciful death.

Death Does Not Decide, Leaving the Matter in the Hands of God

After the interventions by the Indian characters, Death recognizes that the plaintiffs are right: they do not deserve to be treated with such brutality. However, Death then puts forward a biblically based theory about the transcendental necessity of suffering, wars, and evil in the world and says that in any case, those who cause such evil will be punished in the afterlife (321–30). The Indians must, according to Death, patiently bear their suffering as if it were nothing because God, the great shepherd, has already saved them, allowing them into his Church. It is he who will liberate them from these colonial "marauding wolves." Death asks that the Indians, in the meantime, serve God and beware of the tyrants who besiege them (331–50).

The Saints Agree with Death

After Death leaves the case in God's hands, the saints intervene to condemn colonial greed and recommend patience and trust in God. Saint Augustine quotes the scriptures to support his suggestion: until the divine judgment comes, there is nothing else to do but keep working and suffering, for a time will come "when no man can work" (351–60). Saint Dominic prescribes the word of God Almighty, the best medicine (361–65), and Saint Francis tells the Indians that since they are already drinking from Christ's divine fountain, they have the ultimate medicine for all suffering. He also urges them to practice charity, the foremost Franciscan virtue. Saint Francis ends by lamenting that the Indies have so much gold, which is the cause of incurable perdition "among us" (366–80). Saint Dominic states that the colonial heirs will inherit not only the riches, the gold, and the mines, but also eternal damnation (381–90), but his initial countercolonial position collapses after line 391: the saint rhetorically interrogates the Indies' "abyss of sinfulness," asking why they showed their metals, corrupting an unfortunate Europe (391–410). By blaming the Indies, Saint Dominic becomes an anti-Lascasian voice.

Satan and His Companions, Flesh and World, Close the Case

Satan enters the scene to state that he cannot believe some people think they can stop others from going to the Indies. He presents them with a colonial reality check: where, he asks, would people go looking for gold if not there? And, more importantly, where would the Church that proposes such a thing get its income (411–20)?

Gold, says Satan, is a powerful magnet. Flesh cannot agree more: the world is full of wealth and dreams, and nobody has to stay poor in Europe when there is so much to gain in the New World. Flesh adds an androcentric comment: women's conspicuous consumption and expenses are enough to drive their husbands to the Indies just so they can pay the bills (421–40). World argues that the best motive for the colonialist adventurers in the New World is freedom: freedom from wives, children, and laws, for a life of pleasure and well-being. Flesh has the honor of closing Carvajal's *Complaint of the Indians:* in the Indies—unlike in Europe—she says, people can make a good living; that is why all who return to Europe are dying to go back to the New World (441–50).

4. Las Casas Staged

Carvajal's *Complaint of the Indians* evidences the clear influence of Bartolomé de las Casas's political thought, particularly his famous *Brevísima relación de la destruición de las Indias* (Brief History of the Destruction of the Indies), written in 1542 but not published until 1552, five years before Carvajal's work.[59]

A champion of the indigenous cause since 1515, Las Casas had lobbied intensely for the promulgations of the New Laws of 1542, which were intended to hinder the abuses of the encomenderos. Law 30 was perhaps the paramount achievement of the New Laws; it prohibited the inheritance, sale, donation, or other transference of encomienda properties. Between 1542 and 1545, opposition to these New Laws in the New World, as well as lack of enforcement by the authorities and the absence of political will on the part of the emperor, rendered some of the more important provisions ineffective. And in the Royal Provision of October 20, 1545, Charles V reversed Law 30.[60] *Complaint of the Indians* references this victory of the encomenderos and their heirs in lines 181–90.

By 1545, Las Casas understood that the New Laws were unable to protect the Indians from unwarranted wars and servitude.

59. Las Casas, *Brevísima relación de la destruición de las Indias* (Madrid: Tecnos, 1992).

60. Richard Konetzke, *Colección de documentos para la historia de la formación social de Hispanoamérica, 1493–1810*, vol. 1 (Madrid: Consejo Superior de Investigaciones Científicas, 1953), 236–37.

Consequently, he renewed his cause in a return to Spain in 1547, initiating a campaign that resulted in the emperor's moratorium on all new conquests and prohibition of unrecompensed labor (1549), several decrees protecting the Indians, the famous Debate of Valladolid ordered by Charles V (1550–51), and Las Casas's publishing marathon of 1552. Of particular importance to Carvajal's *Complaint of the Indians* are the Debate of 1550–51 and the *Tratados* (Treatises) of 1552.[61]

Las Casas was one of the principal protagonists in the famous Debate of Valladolid, where he refuted his antagonist Juan Ginés de Sepúlveda.[62] The debate before the Junta de Valladolid was initially limited to two central issues. As explained by Fray Domingo de Soto in his summary of the deliberations, the *junta* was first "to inquire into and develop the forms and laws to preach and promote our Holy Catholic Faith in the New World that God has discovered to us," and second, to "examine how those peoples may be subjected to His Majesty the Emperor, Our Lord, without damage to his royal conscience, according to the [*Inter Caetera*] Bull of [Pope] Alexander [VI]."[63] However, Las Casas pushed the debate beyond its initial purpose, turning it into a dispute about "whether it is lawful for His Majesty to make war on those Indians before preaching the faith to them, in order to subject them to his empire, so that, once subjugated, they can be more effectively and easily instructed and enlightened by the evangelical doctrine, becoming aware of their errors as well as of the Christian truth."[64] *Complaint of the Indians* symbolically revisits these questions and also mirrors the historical inconclusiveness of the debate.[65] In addition to this historical correspondence (to which we will return), Carvajal's text contains other distinguishable Lascasian elements, such as a fervent denunciation of the cruelties wrought by the conquistadors and the encomenderos, scorn for the idolatrous colonial appetite for gold (characterized as an evil hunger for human blood), a pacifist condemnation of wars, and

61. Las Casas, *Tratados de Fray Bartolomé de las Casas* (Mexico City: Fondo de Cultura Económica, 1965).

62. See Juan Ginés de Sepúlveda and Bartolomé de las Casas, *Apología*, ed. Ángel Losada (Madrid: Editora Nacional, 1975).

63. Las Casas, "Tratado tercero," in Las Casas, *Tratados*, 228–29.

64. Ibid., 229.

65. There is no known definite formal verdict of the debate; there seem to be only three known opinions by the members of the *junta*. Rolena Adorno, "Los debates sobre la naturaleza del indio en el siglo XVI," *Revista de estudios hispánicos* 9 (1992): 50.

an appeal for the peaceful and voluntary conversion of the native inhabitants of the New World.

Wolves, Gold, and Blood

Complaint of the Indians incessantly reproaches the cruelty and avarice of the conquistadors and encomenderos, utilizing the same harsh metaphors that Las Casas does, and in many instances the same words. For instance, their actions are identified as killings, robberies (34), "fierce and terrible events" (43), and unspeakable "cruelties" (48). They are characterized as famished "giants" (79), "bestial people" (88), "ruthless tyrants" (109, 344) of "sick" and "beastlike hunger" (86, 148). They are rapists (106–9) and vicious murderers (111–20) who will be damned for their greediness (151–60). They are deceitful Christians (166–73), committing crimes that not even barbarians would tolerate (178), worshippers and idolaters of gold and silver (181–85), who instead of disseminating the Word of Christ act like a "plundering" demonic legion (229). They embody the "corruption of virtue and all the laws" (234–35) and offend God beyond comprehensible limits (239–40). They are "perverse" (243) and aggressive people (260) who without provocation inflict war on the Indians (271–80), establishing butcheries (274) to appease an insatiable "thirst" for wealth (280–90). They are "marauding wolves" (340) and a "pestilence for the soul" (347), etc. Carvajal's *Complaint of the Indians* dramatizes Lascasian denunciations. The chieftain, like Las Casas, laments the pillage and rape of Indian women[66] (see 106–10), the mutilation[67] and torture of his people through "murder and fire" (among other methods)[68] (42), and he profusely quotes the Lascasian motifs of cruel carnage, tearing, and dismemberment:

---

66. "Honor" occupies a cardinal place in the Lascasian allegations as well as in *The Court of Death*. See note to line 108.

67. Las Casas cites friar Marcos de Niza: "I affirm that I myself saw before my very eyes the Spaniards cutting hands, noses, ears of Indian men and women" [Yo afirmo que yo mesmo vi ante mis ojos a los españoles cortar manos, narices, orejas a indios y a indias] (Las Casas, *Brevísima*, 129).

68. "They bound the whole body with dry hay, setting them on fire and burning them. . . . They made grills out of rods over forked props and they tied them to them and put a low fire under them so that, little by little, amidst their screams of desperate torment, their souls would leave them" [Liaban todo el cuerpo de paja seca,

To snatch away golden rings
What fingers did they not sever?
What ears did their knives not slash
For the sake of golden earrings?
What arms did they not break?
What wombs, amid cries of woe,
Did they not pierce with their swords?

(111–17)

Faithful to Lascasian discourse, the Indian characters express their
sorrow for those who have been slaughtered and level accusations
against the colonial "butchers,"[69] who, according to Las Casas, "have
done nothing else [with the peoples of the New World] but rip them
to pieces, kill them, anguish them, afflict them, torment them, and
destroy them."[70] The chieftain is pained by the brutality of the conquistadors' vicious games (which Las Casas had denounced[71]), such
as "their daring to take for their target / Human beings" (236–37).
Martyrdom and sacrifice are among the most evident Lascasian
motifs in Complaint of the Indians. Without proposing an explicit
simile, these images support lexical and theological parallels with
Christ's sacrifice. Placing the Indian in the same lexical field as
Christ, Las Casas endows him with the characteristics of a docile
"lamb" and "victim" of an almost Eucharistic sacrifice: "and the
innocent lambs suffered . . . and served with all of their strength, so
one could not help but adore them."[72] In consonance with the metaphor of the pastor/shepherd—which defines the Church and the
empire—the Dominican friar typifies these Indians as "very tame

---

pegándoles fuego así los quemaban. . . . Hacían unas parrillas de varas sobre horquetas
y atábanlos en ellas y poníanles por debajo fuego manso para que, poco a poco, dando
alaridos en aquellos tormentos desesperados, se les salían las animas] (ibid., 23).

69. "Insignes carniceros" (ibid., 133).

70. "Otra cosa no han hecho sino despedazallas, matallas, angustiallas, afligillas,
atormentallas, y destruillas" (ibid., 16–17).

71. Las Casas tells how the conquistadors "made bets about who with one stab
would open the man down the middle or would cut off his head with one chop or
would reveal his entrails" [hacían apuestas sobre quién de una cuchillada abría el
hombre por medio o le cortaba la cabeza de un piquete o le descubría las entrañas]
(ibid., 22).

72. "Y los inocentes corderos sufrieron . . . e servían con todas sus fuerzas, que
no faltaba sino adorallos" (ibid., 68).

lambs" and "sheep," sacrificed in slaughters such as the Cholula massacre.[73] The biblical echoes are fundamental: according to Las Casas, those evil Christians were hungry wolves among innocent lambs and had inverted, and thus perverted, the command of Christ to his disciples to go and preach like sheep among wolves (Matthew 7:15 and 10:16). Contrary to the evangelical mandate, these Christians acted "like the most cruel wolves and tigers and lions hungry from many days of famine" and like "rabid wolves, famished and cruel among sheep or lambs."[74]

Las Casas pleads to the Crown "to free them from the tyranny and perdition they suffer, as if from the mouths of dragons, so that they do not completely consume them."[75] The Indians of the play make that same petition to Death: "To wrest away the control / From these human beasts of prey" and to free them "from such tyranny" (314–15, 320). While Death does not resolve the case, she sympathizes with the plaintiffs and reiterates precisely the tropes of the shepherd, the flock, and the voracious appetite of the tyrants, whom she calls "marauding wolves" (340), the same metaphor that the friar had used to condemn the exploitation of Indian labor and the plundering of the Indies.[76]

73. Ibid., 54–55; see also Las Casas, *Del único modo de atraer a todos los pueblos a la verdadera religión* [*De unico vocationis modo omnium gentium ad veram religionem*], trans. from Latin by Atenógenes Santamaría (Mexico City: Fondo de Cultura Económica, 1975), 190–95. "The Spaniards," Las Casas declares, "organize public *slaughters* of human flesh to feed the dogs as if it were the meat of pork" (*Brevísima*, 143; emphasis added) and even encouraged their indigenous allies to cannibalize other Indians. Pedro de Alvarado, "when he was going to wage war against some towns and provinces, used to take as many of the already subjugated Indians as he could to wage war against the others; and as he did not give anything to eat to the ten [or] twenty thousand men he was taking with him, he obliged them to eat the Indians they took as prisoners" [cuando iba a hacer la Guerra a algunos pueblos y provincias, llevaba de los ya sojuzgados indios cuantos podía que hiciesen la Guerra a los otros; e como no les daba de comer a diez y a veinte mil hombres que llevaba, consentíales que comiesen a los indios que tomaban] (ibid., 70).

74. "Como lobos e tigres y leones crudelísimos de muchos días hambrientos" (Las Casas, *Brevísima*, 16); "lobos rabiosos, famélicos y crueles entre ovejas o corderos" (Las Casas, *Del único modo*, 429). In regard to the conquest of Venezuela, he says: "They entered . . . more irrationally and furiously than the most cruel tigers and than rabid wolves and lions" [Entraron . . . más irracional e furiosamente que crudelísimos tigres y que rabiosos lobos y leones] (*Brevísima*, 106; see also 138).

75. "Librarlos de la tiranía y perdición que padecen, como de la boca de los dragones, y que totalmente no los consuman" (Las Casas, *Entre los remedios*, 643).

76. On Death being a woman, see note 44 to the play.

Throughout his works, Las Casas makes recurring use of the trope of the colonial appetite for blood and of the metonymy that associates wealth with the battered bodies that produce it. The conquistador, he explains, gets "rich off the sweat, blood, and anguish of so many men and peoples" in their servitude.[77] The source of their revenue, he declares, was "squeezed from the blood of the Indians that they had killed and were killing over there."[78] The Christians committed "great abuses and sins . . . oppressing and tormenting and mistreating [the Indians] in the mines and in other jobs, until they had *consumed* and finished off all of those miserable innocents"[79] (emphasis added). And he asks, "To what Christian man's mind could it occur [that these] innocents were handed over [to them] so that they could take from their blood the riches they hold as their

77. "Rico de los sudores, sangre y angustias de tantos hombres y gentes." Las Casas, *Historia de las Indias*, ed. André Saint-Lu, 3 vols. (Caracas: Biblioteca Ayacucho, 1986), 3:79. Faced with the extinction of the native population of the Caribbean, the Dominican fathers of La Española sent a letter to Charles V (December 4, 1519) vehemently denouncing the brutality of the conquistadors and the injustice of the encomienda system. They brand the encomenderos as "butchers" and the slave-trade expeditions in the Caribbean "butcheries," just as in the play (274). The letter identifies the opulence and richness of colonial commodities with the bodies whose exploitation produced European wealth: American goods and wealth were soaked in blood and attained at the expense of the innumerable human lives consumed by the encomenderos. See the complete letter in Joaquín Francisco Pacheco et al., eds., *Colección de documentos inéditos, relativos al descubrimiento, conquista y organización de las antiguas posesiones españolas de América y Oceanía*, vol. 35 (Madrid: Ministerio de ultramar, 1875), 199–240.

78. "De la sangre de los indios que allí habían muerto y mataban, exprimían" (Las Casas, *Historia de las Indias*, 3:333).

79. "Grandes insultos y pecados . . . oprimiendo y atormentando y vejando en las minas y en los otros trabajos, hasta *consumir* y acabar todos aquellos infelices inocentes" (Las Casas, *Brevísima*, 34; emphasis added). The conquest is presented, over and over again, as the slaughter and consumption of innocents: "The people of the island of San Juan, seeing that they were on the path to being *consumed* . . . decided to defend themselves" [viendo las gentes de la isla de San Juan que llevaban el camino par ser *consumidos* . . . acordaron de se defender] (*Historia de las Indias*, 2:202; emphasis added); "By that time, the year 1516, the Spaniards did not forget that they were guilty of *consuming* the docile people of the island of Cuba" [Por ese tiempo y año de 1516, no olvidaban los españoles que tenían cargo de consumir la gente mansísima de la isla de Cuba] (ibid., 3:333; emphasis added). The Spaniards "were into these so inhumane *slaughters* for nearly seven years. . . . Just estimate the number of people they managed to *consume*" [Estuvieron (los españoles) en estas *carnicerías* tan inhumanas cerca de siete años. . . . Júzguese *cuánto sería el número de la gente que consumirían*] (*Brevísima*, 68; emphasis added).

god?"[80] Worshipping gold is for Las Casas "also an idolatry," for it replaces God with metals and worldly wealth.[81] *Complaint of the Indians* echoes Lascasian discourse in order to articulate a Christian critique of the "ambition and diabolic greed" that drove the exploits of the New World.[82] The Europeans' "worship" of riches copiously sacrifices innocent blood; it is—as the chieftain maintains—an idolatry for which its faithful would steal from "even Christ Himself" (181–85).

In Lascasian discourse, the verb "to consume" ("consumir") is not metaphorically associated with the voracious "savage," but rather with the wolf-conquistador. Las Casas equates the "hunger" for gold with both idolatry and the rapacious appetite for blood. Note that for him "consumir" has the double meaning of annihilation and communion.[83] In fact, the word is defined by Covarrubias (1611) as the "act of taking the priest, the body of our Lord Christ, on the bread and the wine, during the holy sacrifice of Mass."[84] When Las Casas states that the encomenderos "consume the Indians," his trope depicts the colonial consumption of labor as a diabolic distortion of the Eucharist. The hermeneutic key to the sacrifice and colonial consumption of the indigenous is, again, the evangelical paradox: the encomenderos' "consumption" is a perverse communion. The body of the innocent lamb-Indian—semantically close to that of Christ— is both sacrificed and consumed in the impious religion of gold; that is, in the idolatry of the Devil. The joy of communion thus turns to bitterness and the martyrdom is left unredeemed. An indigenous character in the play articulates precisely the inherent contradiction

---

80. "¿En qué juicio de hombre cristiano pudo caber . . . [que] les entregasen los inocentes para que de su sangre sacasen las riquezas que tienen por su dios?" (Las Casas, *Entre los remedios*, 673).

81. Las Casas, *Del único modo*, 374.

82. Las Casas, *Brevísima*, 61.

83. The examples of this use of *consumir* are abundant in the *Brevísima*: "other killing and thieving tyrants followed, who were to *consume* the peoples" [sucedieron otros tiranos matadores y robadores, que fueron a *consumir* las gentes] (90); "they finish them off and *consume* them in a few days . . . they finished *consuming* all of the Lucayo Indians that there were in these islands when the Spaniards fell into this profit" [los acaban e *consumen* en breves días . . . acabaron de *consumir* a todos los indios lucayos que había en estas islas cuando cayeron los españoles en esta granjería] (104), etc.

84. Sebastián de Covarrubias, *Tesoro de la lengua castellana o Española* (Barcelona: S.A. Horta, I. E., 1943), s.v. "consumir."

within these two communions or consumptions: "these people promise you wine / And sell you nothing but vinegar, / Exploiting hour by hour / The poor and suffering Indian" (172–75).

Radical Pacifism and the Debate over (Un)Just War

The Debate of Valladolid between Sepúlveda and Las Casas (1550–51) centered on a fundamental dispute related to the justice or injustice of war as a means of fulfilling the evangelical mission proposed in the pontifical decrees (the *Inter-caetera, Eximiae Devotionis*, and second *Inter-caetera* bulls, 1493).[85] As stated above, *Complaint of the Indians* symbolically paralleled this debate in many respects. According to De Soto's summary, Sepúlveda rationalized war against the Indians as lawful for four reasons: (1) because of the sins which the Indians had committed, especially their idolatries, and their sins against nature; (2) because of the rudeness of their nature, which obliged them to serve the Spaniards; (3) in order to spread the Christian faith, a task that would be more easily accomplished through the prior subjugation of the natives; and (4) to protect the innocents among the natives themselves from unjust injuries and sacrifices.[86] Refuting Sepúlveda's first argument, Las Casas argued that even if the Indians were committing crimes (which they were not), it was not lawful for the Spaniards to punish them since the Spaniards had no jurisdiction over the unconquered Indians. It was up to their kings and chieftains to punish those criminals. In *Complaint of the Indians*, the Indian characters respond with irony to the kind of colonial justification maintained by Sepúlveda, which for them is unintelligible. Carvajal's Indians understand neither the argument of the conquest as punishment nor what they call the "mystery" of imperial colonial sovereignty (301–10); as they sarcastically state, they "must be just too blind to see" ("como andamos con candiles"). On these points, the characters not only generally coincide with Las Casas, they also adopt the juridical doctrine of the theologian Francisco de Vitoria (ca. 1492–1546) on this same matter.

85. The bulls of Pope Alexander VI (1493) justified the title of territorial property for discovered lands with an evangelizing finality. For the text of the bulls see the appendix to Las Casas, *Tratados*, 2:1277–90.
86. See Lewis Hanke, *The Spanish Struggle for Justice in the Conquest of America* (Philadelphia: University of Pennsylvania Press, 1949), especially chap. 8.

Vitoria had countered the theses under which a Christian prince could punish another for being a pagan or the pope could order and sustain a just war against those who committed "barbarous sins against nature."[87] In accordance with the iusnaturalist thesis of Saint Thomas, Vitoria maintained that sin does not deprive humans of their inherent rights: on their own land, the barbarians should not be forced to abide by foreign laws, however just these may be, nor to comply with the divine law that has not been revealed to them. In *De Indis*, Vitoria affirms that "not even by the authority of the pope can the Christian princes separate the Indians by force from sins against nature, nor [can they] punish them for [those sins]."[88] Like Las Casas, Vitoria did not believe that the Indians' sins or their rejection of the Catholic faith excused the extremes of war. Furthermore, he did not believe that the despoilment of riches could be justified by the supposed absence of property among the Indians.[89]

Sepúlveda's second argument was that war against the Indians was lawful due to their natural condition as barbarians, a status that presupposed their need for governance under a people more civilized than themselves.[90] Las Casas refuted Sepúlveda in his definition of the term "barbarian." According to Las Casas, there are four uses of the term: cruel people; linguistic barbarians (as in its original meaning, a non-Greek speaker); barbarians in the strict Aristotelian sense of the word (i.e., those incapable of governing themselves, considered by Aristotle natural slaves); and religious barbarians

---

87. Francisco de Vitoria, *De temperentia* (1537), in *Escritos políticos*, ed. Luciano Pereña (Buenos Aires: Ediciones Depalma, 1967), 258–63.

88. Francisco de Vitoria, *De Indis* (1539), in *Doctrina sobre los indios*, trans. and ed. Ramón Hernández Martín (Salamanca: Editorial San Esteban, 1992), 133.

89. Ibid., 103–32. Despite the long tradition that invoked the absence of property among the aboriginals, Vitoria begins with the opposite presupposition, declaring the right to property as a universal right, independent of the sins of the title-bearer.

90. Losada and Adorno indicate that Las Casas distorted Sepúlveda's argument about the *natural* inferiority of the Indians. Sepúlveda did not question the humanity of the Indians, nor did he claim that the Indians were inherently slaves because their inferiority. Sepúlveda was talking about a form of servitude he extrapolated from Aristotle to feudal relations and to the encomienda regime. Las Casas's "distortion" was a selective, and highly strategic, reading of Sepúlveda's argument. Ángel Losada, ed., introduction to *Apología*, by Juan Ginés de Sepúlveda and Bartolomé de las Casas (Madrid: Editora Nacional, 1975); Adorno, "Los debates sobre la naturaleza del indio en el siglo XVI." See also Lewis Hanke's classic study *Aristotle and the American Indians: A Study in Race Prejudice in the Modern World* (London: Hollis and Carter, 1959).

(non-Christians). For Las Casas, the Indians could only be considered barbarians linguistically and religiously, neither of which justifies war. Likewise, the Indians in the play are not barbarous or cruel, but rather the peaceful victims of countless cruelties (e.g., 26, 35, 41–45, 48, 101–20). Because they speak Spanish and are Christian, they are not barbarians even in the linguistic or religious sense; therefore, wars against them are unjustifiable.

Sepúlveda's third argument was that war was a means of evangelization. Las Casas contested this in his affirmation, noted above, that war alienated the Indians through pernicious acts that contradicted the very pastoral purpose of evangelization. In the play, the Indian characters repeatedly draw attention to the hypocritical nature of a Christian doctrine that decrees salvation in the shadow of the violent and rapacious actions of its "pseudo-preachers," as Las Casas calls them.[91] According to the friar, because of the self-proclaimed "evangelizing wars," the natives become fearful and apprehensive; they learn to hate Spaniards and flee from them, thus impeding their reception of the Holy Word. A chieftain describes the situation in precise and similar terms: "We came to the hard decision / To leave our lands" and escape to "Distant, deserted places / Far from the exhaustion of war" (186–90). Here, as in many other instances, Carvajal follows Las Casas, who contemplates the Indian exodus (the Indians "fleeing to the mountains").[92] Instead of the Indians being attracted by Christian ideals, war meant that they constantly "fled to the mountains to get away from such merciless people."[93]

Sepúlveda's fourth argument in support of the war against the Indians declared the obligation of the Spanish to protect the innocent. In this he followed one of Vitoria's justifications:[94] "Another

91. Las Casas, *El único modo*, 398.
92. Las Casas, "Sobre la destrucción de los indios," in *Obras completas*, 13:243 (Madrid: Alianza, 1998) (*Obras completas* cited hereafter as *OC*).
93. "Huíanse a los montes por apartarse de gente tan dura" (Las Casas, *Brevísima*, 22).
94. Vitoria's other justifications included the natural right to transit; "natural sociability and communication" among all humans; the right to hospitality; the exercise of the *ius negotiandi* or the right to commerce; the right of the Spaniards to defend themselves against attacks or aggressions from the indigenous; the right to preach the faith by divine mandate (Vitoria, *De Indis*, 136–43); and the fulfillment of obligations to the Indians who were "associates or friends" (145).

title could be established due to the tyranny of the Indian lords themselves . . . because they sacrifice innocent men or because they kill them in order to eat them, etc. I affirm that, even without the authority of the pope, Spaniards can defend the innocent from unjust death."[95] In other words, what constitutes the just cause of colonial intervention is not the sin, albeit abominable, nor the infringement of natural law itself, but rather the biblical mandate to protect the innocent (Proverbs 24:11–12), the victims of human sacrifice.[96] For Las Casas, however, wars create more victims than souls saved. The friar restates the question of the "protection of the innocent" in a manner distinct from that of Vitoria and Sepúlveda: the innocent must be protected, indeed, but not from the local indigenous "tyrants" and their idolatrous sacrifices, but rather from the Spaniards. Las Casas envisions an empire that shelters the Indians from "the vehement and diabolical tyranny of those despicable tyrants"[97]—the "ruthless tyrants" from whom the Indian characters of the play desire protection (109, 344) and against whom, at one point, they contemplate rebellion (141–50).

Las Casas finds no acceptable motive for the wars against the Indians: not their infidelity, not their crimes, not their alleged

95. Ibid., 144. This is the same argument Vitoria had elaborated before, in *De temperantia*: "It is licit to defend the innocent even if he does not ask for it; what is more, even if he refuses [to be defended], especially since he suffers an injustice in which he cannot cede his right. . . . No one can give another the right to kill him, or to devour him. . . . So it is licit to defend them. . . . Therefore the reason by virtue of which the barbarians can be punished with war is not because the eating of human flesh or sacrificing of men goes against natural law, but rather because [these practices] cause men to be hurt" (265–66; emphasis added).

96. Other jurists, such as Melchor Cano (1509–60), Diego de Covarrubias (1512–77), and Juan de la Peña, would argue in the same vein. Cano, in opposition to the thesis of natural slavery argued by Sepúlveda, sustained the right to intervention—not "of justice, but rather of charity"—in order to protect the Indians dominated by the tyrants who "commit crimes in detriment to the innocent [such as] eating human flesh, [and] sacrificing men to the gods." Melchor Cano, "Dominio sobre los indios," in Pereña, *Misión de España en América, 1540–1560*, 109–10. Covarrubias opined in a similar manner: "It can be the cause of a just war against the Indians to lend help to various innocents who are sacrificed and killed every year." Diego de Covarrubias, "Justicia de la guerra contra los indios," in Pereña, *Misión de España en América, 1540–1560*, 186, 221. For Peña, "those who kill men in order to eat them, as the cannibals do among the Indians, [can] be punished by war. . . . This war is in *defense of the innocent*" (emphasis added). Juan de la Peña, "¿Es justa la guerra contra los indios?" in Pereña, *Misión de España en América, 1540–1560*, 287.

97. "La tiranía de aquellos infelices tiranos . . . vehemente e diabólica" (Las Casas, *Brevísima*, 140).

inferiority, and certainly not an offensive provocation on their part.
Both Las Casas in *Tratados* and the chieftain in Carvajal's work
affirm that the Indians provide no reason for bellicose action.[98] The
chieftain, for example, justly asks:

> What harm or what evil turn,
> What insult or what dishonor
> Are we responsible for,
> To account for such a butchery
> As these people bring on our heads?
> Did we by some chance despoil
> Their fields, their patrimonies,
> Their wives? What madness
> Is this, what is the tragic cause
> For this hatred without end?
>
> (271–80)

In a letter to an unknown person in the Spanish court in 1535,
Las Casas condensed what would be a recurrent indictment in his
writings: "these infidels do not . . . leave their lands to rob us or to
infest ours, but rather we are those who come to invade and dispos-
sess their lands. . . . We take their women and children and leave
them not even a simple pot as property. And we place them and
their people in an infernal captivity."[99] Therefore, if there is any
justification for war, it is that of the Indians against the tyrants who
oppress them (see below, Section 5).

As discussed above, Carvajal's *Complaint of the Indians* alludes
to the theories of war discussed in the Debate of Valladolid and Las
Casas's *Tratados*, but in a general sense the play appeals to a radical
Christian pacifism. In *De unico vocationis modo omnium gentium*

---

98. Las Casas states, for example: "This tyrant [Francisco de Montejo] . . .
began to wage cruel wars against those good, innocent people, who were in their
houses without offending anyone" [Comenzó este tirano . . . a hacer crueles guerras a aquellas gentes buenas, inocentes, que estaban en sus casas sin ofender a nadie]
(ibid., 78).

99. "[E]stos infieles no . . . salen de sus tierras para irnos a robar o a infestar,
antes nosotros venimos e invadimos las suyas, los echamos de ellas. . . . Les tomamos
sus mujeres e hijos y no les dejamos uno sola olla que sea suya. . . . Y a sus mismas
personas, con todos los que les tocan, ponemos en infernal cautiverio." Las Casas,
"Carta a un personaje de la corte," in *OC*, 13:93.

ad veram religionem (1537), Las Casas contends that war against the Indians for the simple fact of their infidelity or religious difference became "unjust and tyrannical."[100] He instead proposes the "persuasion of understanding by means of reason and gentle inclination of will."[101] Likewise, *Complaint of the Indians* favors the peaceful conversion of the Indians advocated by the Dominican friar. The initial monologue of the chieftain first announces that the complainants are already Christians. He specifically states that the power of preaching (*predicación*)—not war—has resulted in their conversion to Catholicism: "By the simple path of the Word" (14). In any case, the actual purpose of the wars against the Indians, as stated by Las Casas, the Indian characters, and the saints in the play, is not to spread the Word, but to satisfy a deep and malevolent greed (45, 74, 75, 80, 85–95, 111–20, 145–65, 181–85, 224, 225, 238, 281–90, 371–410). In the last part of the play, even Satan states that gold is the real magnet that attracts Europeans to the New World (401–10). If evangelical war is inherently unjust, then the war against the Indians— which under the false pretext of Christianity finds its true motivation in an "insatiable avarice" (75)—is even more perverse and evil. The chieftain underlines the pervasive effect of war and greed on the evangelization of the New World: Christianity brought salvation but also the evil of these hypocritical and false "Christians" (20–25, 36–45). While the Indians used to adore silent and idol gods, says the chieftain, "Not one disturbed us at all, / Not one came to kill or rob us, / Or wage cruel warfare upon us" (33–35). But having converted to Christianity, he continues, the Indians suffer infinite tyrannies, insults, cruelties, and injustices (28–45).

Of course this complaint is related to the numerous and ineffective provisions that exempted the converted indigenous peoples from

---

100. "It is a frightening, unjust and tyrannical war that . . . is declared against the infidels—who never have known anything about the Faith, nor the Church, nor have offended in any way that same Church—with the only objective of, once subjugated to the dominion of the Christians by that same war, preparing their souls to receive the Faith or the Christian religion" [Es temeraria, injusta y tiránica la guerra que . . . a los infieles que nunca han sabido nada acerca de la Fe, ni de la Iglesia, ni han ofendido de ningún modo a la misma Iglesia, se les declara con el solo objeto de que, sometidos al imperio de los cristianos por medio de la misma guerra, preparen sus ánimos para recibir la Fe o la religión cristiana]. Las Casas, *Del único modo*, 422.

101. "Persuasión del entendimiento por medio de razones y suave moción de la voluntad" (ibid., 65). Although *De unico vocationis modo* was not published until 1942, its ideas permeated other writings by the friar and were known and commonly cited (see Lewis Hanke's introduction to *Del único modo*, 23).

war and servitude; provisions that were systematically ignored in a colonial system deeply rooted in the exploitation of forced indigenous labor. Conversion, in most circumstances, did not guarantee a religious refuge: "we can find / No king or champion to help us," the chieftain says (6–7). Mistreatment of the native convert would be another of the numerous evangelical paradoxes incorporated into the writings of both Las Casas and Carvajal. One of the indigenous characters paraphrases the Bible (Matthew 20:8 and Luke 13:29–30) to lament the difference between early Christianity (the converted pagan Europe) and the Christianity of the New World, which arrived "late" to the "Lord's vineyard" (121–30). According to the scriptures (a subtext that informs both the Indians' allegations in *Complaint of the Indians* and Las Casas's denunciations), God seats everyone at his table, from the last unto the first, but the Christians who have come to the Indies do not: they discriminate against and oppress the latecomers and wage cruel and unjust wars against them.[102]

102. Juan A. Ortega y Medina supposes that Carvajal himself might have been a New Christian, based on the genealogy of his last name. Likewise, Alfredo Hermenegildo suggests that the author could have been a descendent of *conversos*, based on some textual markers in the *Tragedia Josephina* studied by David Gitlitz, such as the distinction between two kinds of Jewish characters: the evil ones (brothers of Joseph), who use the singular "Dio," and others, such as Joseph himself, who refer to "Dios" (plural). The plural supposes a prefiguration of conversion and acceptance of the mystery of the Holy Trinity. Hermenegildo argues that with this double perspective, Jews belonging to the Christian tradition can be distinguished from the Other-Jews (43); the latter category would include the Jews of *The Court of Death* who, in effect, use the form "Dio." Alfredo Hermenegildo, "Política, sociedad y teatro religioso del siglo XVI" *Criticón*, nos. 94–95 (2005): 43. On this matter, consult David Gitlitz's well-informed studies, especially "Carvajal's *Cortes de la Muerte*: La actitud cristiano-nueva en *Las Cortes de la Muerte*," *Segismundo* 9 (1974): 141–64, where, based on a detailed genealogical study, he concludes that it is at least possible that Miguel de Carvajal (the insolvent) came from a family of New Christians on his mother's side. Independently of Carvajal's ancestry, the converted "savages" of *Complaint of the Indians* parallel the experiences of converted Jews and New Christians in Spain. This implicit connection would have been clearly noticeable to readers and spectators in the second part of the fifteenth century. It must be noted that in Scene XX of *The Court of Death*—following the grievance of the Indians—two groups of litigants come before Death, a group of Moors and another of Jews (fols. 54v–61v), and here the Jews themselves lament their misfortunes in Spain. The Jews of Scene XX are not *conversos* (as the Indians are); consequently, the argument about the equality of *conversos* (as a general principle) is not formulated expressly in the scene of the Jews, but rather in that of the Indians. The Jewish characters reject Christianity and therefore must reluctantly depart for exile. Although other parts of the text express a certain anti-Semitism, this scene reveals a poetic sympathy for the outcasts (fol. 55r). See note to line 122 of the play.

Both *Complaint of the Indians* and Las Casas's work condemn the wars in America in terms similar to those in Erasmus's anti-Machiavellian *Institutio principis christiani* (Education of a Christian Prince) (1516), a humanistic portrait of the ideal sovereign, and *Querela pacis* (Complaint of Peace) (1517), a treatise on the evils of war and the pacifist teachings of Christ. As Marcel Bataillon has observed, the adherents of Erasmus in Spain did not intervene in the debate about the just war against the Indians in the New World,[103] but Erasmus's ideas did have an effect. Las Casas's evangelical doctrine on war embraces the Erasmist conviction that violence is an affront to the gospel and that to be true, faith must be free. Erasmus's views also inform the friar's diatribe against what he had calls "strident weapons that go about sowing cadavers all over."[104] For Las Casas, "War brings with it the following evils: the clash of arms; assaults and sudden invasions, impetuous and furious; violence and ominous turmoil; scandals, deaths and slaughters; havoc, plundering and despoilments; the privation of fathers of their sons, and of sons of their fathers."[105] *Complaint of the Indians* grasps the Erasmist and Lascasian maxim on the perniciousness of war (i.e., 35, 190, 251–55, 326–27). One of the complainant Indians asks:

> Whoever saw in our lands
> Muskets, lances, or swords,
> Or any of those inhuman inventions
> Of weapons employed in wars
> To spill blood upon all sides?
>
> (251–55)

For both Las Casas and the Indian characters in Carvajal's play, wars against the Indians were not only vile and repugnant to Christian philosophy, but also an impediment to evangelization; more significantly, they were completely unjustified.

103. Marcel Bataillon, *Erasmo y España: Estudios sobre la historia espiritual del siglo XVI* (Mexico City: Fondo de Cultura Económica, 1996), 86–91, 632–33.

104. "Armas estrepitosas que van sembrando cadáveres por doquiera" (Las Casas, *Del único modo*, 351).

105. "La Guerra trae consigo estos males: el estrépito de las armas; las acometidas e invasiones repentinas, impetuosas y furiosas; las violencias y las graves perturbaciones; los *escándalos,* las muertes y las *carnicerías;* los estragos, las rapiñas, los despojos; el privar a los padres de sus hijos, y a los hijos de sus padres" (ibid., 343).

The reading of *Complaint of the Indians* vis-à-vis Bartolomé de Las Casas clearly illustrates the latter's presence. The aforementioned examples and the notes to this edition highlight that commonality. Yet the Debate of Valladolid and the publications of 1552 (in particular the *Brevísima relación*) represent more than the obvious background of Carvajal's work, which could be characterized to a certain extent as a theatrical rewriting of Las Casas. It is, on the one hand, a Lascasian piece: it employs many of Las Casas's evangelical and political metaphors, displays some of the key elements of his theo-political thought, and stages in part his theories on the (un)just war against the Indians and the evangelical mission of Spain. On the other hand, as we will see in the following section, the play is appallingly anti-Lascasian in its betrayal of Las Casas's efforts to engage the empire in the effective defense and protection of the Indians, eliminate the encomiendas, and ultimately restore the rights of the Indians.

5. Medicine, Insurrection, and Deferred Justice

Las Casas found that the immediate outcome of his campaigns was largely discursive and legalistic: the self-definition of the Spanish Empire as protector of the Indians and a series of legal reforms that regulated the exploitation of Indian labor in the New World. For the most part, these reforms sought to end forced unpaid labor and to control the abuses of Spanish colonists. "The aim, therefore, was to establish a system of voluntary wage labor with moderated tasks; but in anticipation that the Indians might not offer their services voluntarily," the colonial authorities were to "deliver laborers to colonists who needed them," insure the payment of their wages, and require their fair treatment. Justices or *jueces repartidores* summoned the Indian workers and assigned them to labor on farms, in mines, on public works, and in the domestic service of colonial society."[106] In its legal and administrative attempts to regulate Indian labor, the empire did not dismantle the unjust order; rather, it

---

106. Silvio Zavala, "The Evolving Labor System," in *Indian Labor in the Spanish Indies*, ed. John Francis Bannon (Boston: Heath, 1966), 77.

reformed and regulated injustice without disrupting the coloniality[107] of exploitation that Las Casas denounced.

After the Debate of Valladolid, Las Casas himself seemed conscious of his ineffective search for remedy and redress from the Empire. In 1555, he wrote to the famous theologian Bartolomé Carranza, "those innocent people have been plundered, tyrannized and ravaged for more than sixty years; the emperor has ruled Castile for forty years, and he has never given any other remedy [*remedio*] to all these wrongs than patches [*remiendo*] here and there."[108] The contrast that Las Casas draws between "remedio" and "remiendo" underscores the failures of imperial policy for the Indies. "Remedio" refers to "the means implemented to repair some damage," an "amendment or correction," and a "refuge"; it is also a "synonym of legal action" and of "medicine."[109] While in the political context "remedios" is a generic term for governmental remedies, it also references a subgenre of the treatises that provide moral and political instruction for the prince—specifically, those that inform him of the maladies of the kingdom and its subjects, and propose corrective measures that promote upright and effective governance. Las Casas wrote several, including his famous *Memorial de remedios para las Indias* (1516), a utopian plan for the New World, and *Memorial de remedios para las Indias* and *Memorial de remedios para Tierra Firme* (both 1518), which petitioned for the end of raids, cruelties, wars of conquest, and slavery.[110] In *Memorial de remedios* and *Conclusiones sumarias sobre el remedio de las Indias* (both 1542), Las Casas demands the end of encomiendas, forced labor, and conquests, and reiterates the need for the protection of the Indians

107. "Coloniality"—a term that I borrow from Aníbal Quijano—is a global hegemonic model of power in place since the conquest that articulates race and labor. It could be defined as the structure of social relations and practices of domination and exploitation that emerges with the conquest and colonization of the "New World" and continues through the insertion of vast populations into the world-system of the exploitation of labor. The term emphasizes that in the present these relations and practices persist and are reproduced in the constant renewal and renovation of colonialism and oppression.

108. "A sesenta años y uno más que se roban, tiraniçan y asuelan inocentes gentes, y quarenta que reyna el Emperador en Castilla, y nunca las ha remediado sino a remiendos." Las Casas, "Carta al maestro fray Bartolomé Carranza," in *OC*, 13:280.

109. RAE, *Autoridades 1737* (Madrid: F. del Hierro, 1726–37), 564–65.

110. Las Casas, *Memorial de remedios para las Indias* (1516); *Memorial de remedios para las Indias* (1518); *Memorial de remedios para Tierra Firme* (1518).

from tyrannical powers.[111] Later, he entitled one of his 1552 treatises *Entre los remedios*.[112] For Las Casas, there existed one true remedy for the Indies and all others derived from it: the eradication of servitude in the New World, "to take away the power of the Spaniards over the Indians, which means to revoke the encomiendas and *repartimientos*, is the true remedy for so many offenses."[113]

From the Court of Death, the Indians ask for a remedy analogous to that demanded by Las Casas: to strip the tyrants of power through court decree. One of them petitions the court to provide a judgment ("proveer") in opposition to the tyrannical abuses of the encomenderos:

> It only remains to be seen
> If by this honorable court
> A judgment could somehow be found
> To wrest away the control
> From these human beasts of prey.
>
> (311–15)

This dramatic appeal to justice from the empire mirrors Las Casas's relentless plea for the same. In *Memorial de remedios* (1542), the friar declares that the ultimate cure for the Indies originates in the fact "that your Majesty is obligated, by divine law, to take in his royal Crown all the Indians from all the Indies as the free subjects they are and to rescue them from the encomiendas."[114] In a letter to another renowned theologian, Domingo de Soto, in 1549, Las Casas reiterates:

> What great joy your letter brought me, father, and the immense hope to see my work concluded before I die and my wishes for the remedy for those souls accomplished.

111. Las Casas, *Memorial de remedios* (1542); *Conclusiones sumarias sobre el remedio de las Indias* (1542).

112. Las Casas, *Entre los remedios*.

113. "Sacar de poder de los epañoles los yndios, que es revocar todas las encomiendas y repartimientos, sea el verdadero remedio de tantos males" (Las Casas, "Carta al maestro fray Bartolomé Carranza," 286).

114. "Que su Mgst. es obligado de precepto divino a encorporar en su real corona, todos los indios de todas las indias como vasallos libres que son y quitallos de las encomiendas de los xpristianos" (Las Casas, *Memorial de remedios*, 126).

> That remedy consists in your Majesty deciding on two
> things that—if I know anything about the law of Christ—
> he is required to rule as per divine law. The first is to elimi-
> nate the iniquitous conquests that are a disgrace and an
> infamy for the faith. . . . The second is that your Majesty
> fully receive all the Indians under his Crown, destroying
> and eradicating the *repartimiento*.[115]

Strictly speaking, the empire could never offer viable remedies
while its existence depended on the exploitation of the Indies and the
Indians. It could merely restructure colonial domination. In 1554,
three years after the debate, King Philip, then in London, seriously
considered a proposal from Peruvian encomenderos that sought the
perpetual ownership of their encomiendas together with the administrative and court jurisdiction, all of which was equivalent to a feudal
concession. Their offer was five million gold ducats. Tempted in a
moment of deep exhaustion of public finances, Philip summoned
yet another junta to contemplate the encomenderos' proposition;
the junta sustained Philip's initial inclination toward the offer, an
action that Las Casas and others branded as the "sale of Peru and
its Indians." Philip ordered the formation of an executive commis-
sion and the initiation of a plan that conceded the perpetual status
of the encomiendas. The impending transaction confronted strong
resistance from the Council of the Indies, various theologians such as
Bartolomé Carranza, and, of course, Las Casas, who not only opposed
it in his writings but also, as representative of the chieftains of Peru,
put forward a monetary counteroffer to compete with the encomenderos. Furthermore, in his "Memorial sumario a Felipe II" (Brief
Summary to Philip II) (1556), Las Casas argued that the Indians had
to be "summoned, warned, and listened to" ("llamados y avisados y
oídos") on this matter and that Philip "should summon representatives before court and all the states" ("mandase llamar procuradores

---

115. "Grande alegría reçebí con la carta de V.P. y la esperança muy grande de
ver antes que me muera el fin de mis trabajos y deseos cumplidos por el remedio de
aquellas animas, que solo consiste en que su Mag. proveea dos cosas que, si yo se
algo de la ley de Christo, es obligado a proveer de precepto divino. La una es quitar
aquel oprobio e infamia de la fe tan grande que son las iniquíssimas conquistas. . . .
La segunda que su Mag. Incorpore absolutamente en su corona real todos los indios
deshaziendo y anihilando este repartimiento." Las Casas, "Carta a Fray Domingo de
Soto," in *OC*, 13:247.

de Cortes y todos los estados") before deciding on the "sale."[116] Only in the literary imagination of Carvajal was there such an inclusive court as Las Casas proposed. The proposition of the encomenderos was discussed on both sides of the Atlantic for almost ten years without resolution. This example illustrates why a clear and effective *remedio* for the Indies, as Las Casas conceived it, was simply beyond the imperial conditions of possibility, and why after quoting so much of Las Casas, *Complaint of the Indians* has such a colonialist finale. The colonial question was stubbornly material: in no other moment did Spain obtain so much gold from the Indies as during this ten-year period between 1551 and 1560, following the Debate of Valladolid.[117] Discourses against colonial riches and exploitation were mere exercises of moral imagination. Liberation of the Indians was for the most part a speculative matter; remedies were not destined to eliminate oppression but rather to soothe the imperial conscience.

Occasioned by the relative absence of possible imperial remedies, the Indians, Death, and the saints recommend alternative measures. All but quoting Las Casas, Carvajal's Indians, for instance, contemplate their imminent self-exile from the Christians to "seek out / Distant, deserted places / Far from the exhaustion of war" (188–90). Paramount amid these remedies for the colonial devastation of the Indies, the pestilence of war, and the oppression of foreign tyrants is the direct reference to Indian insurrection against their oppressors. Seeking to "quiet the hunger of such insatiable avarice" (74–75), to cure the "burning thirst" for wealth (145) and the colonial "beast-like hunger" for metals (148), the chieftain proposes as "medicine" the pouring of molten gold into the rapacious mouths of the con-quistadors, as allegedly the Parthians did with Marcus Licinius Crassus (115–53 B.C.):[118] "That same medicine is the one / We should certainly use / Against that beastlike hunger" (146–48). Apparently certain Indians put this remedy into practice, as evidenced in the account of Girolamo Benzoni in *La Historia del Mondo Nuovo* (1565): "Because of [their] unlimited cruelty and tyranny, as well as

116. Las Casas, "Memorial sumario a Felipe II," in *OC*, 13:311.

117. Jean-Paul Le Flem, "Los aspectos económicos de la España moderna," in *La frustración de un imperio, 1476–1714*, by Manuel Tuñón de Lara, Jean-Paul Le Flem, and Joseph Perez, vol. 5 of *Historia de España*, ed. Manuel Tuñón de Lara (Barcelona: Labor, 1982), 70.

118. See lines 141–49 and note to line 145 of the play.

the greed of these men, they [the Indians] poured molten gold into the mouths of however many they could trap, but above all into [the mouths of] the captains . . . pronouncing these words: *Eat gold, eat gold, insatiable Christian.*"[119] Teodoro de Bry, Protestant editor and illustrator of Benzoni's book, visually represents this equivalency between cannibalism and the colonialist appetite in a memorable engraving in which the Indians punish a conquistador by making him drink liquid gold in the foreground, while in the background several human extremities are being grilled and eaten: an eloquent visual equation of the appetite for human flesh and the avidity for gold.

Las Casas never proposed one unified theory on tyranny and resistance, but he consistently characterized the colonial exploitation of Indian labor as tyrannical, thus declaring the political and patrimonial "rights" of the conquistadors and encomenderos illegitimate; they were tyrants in usurpation (*tyranni in titula*) and tyrants in oppression (*tyranni in regimine*). Accordingly, Las Casas also supported the right of the Indian subjects (as members of Christendom and the empire) to resist those tyrants, in accordance with the political theory of the day.[120] This matter, of course, proved both sensitive and divided; most Spanish thinkers recognized this right of rebellion for the subjects of other states, but not for the Catalonians, the Moriscos, the Comuneros, the Flemish, or the Indians. This political ambivalence structures the logic of the play; after all, the character who proposes to emulate the Parthian punishment of Crassus does not, in the end, wage a countercolonial war, but instead presents himself at the Court of Death, just as Las Casas worked within the legal framework by lobbying and petitioning the empire. Insurrection, then, is the very real but elusive specter behind both the legal and dramatic representation of the injustice of the conquest and exploitation of the New World.

119. Girolamo Benzoni, *La Historia del Mondo Nuovo*, in *América de Bry, 1590–1634*, by Teodoro de Bry, ed. Gereon Sievernich (Madrid: Siruela, 1992), 177.

120. The prevailing theological doctrine from the Middle Ages was the justification for rebellion (or at least resistance) against oppressive rulers (Thomas Aquinas, *Summa Theologiae* II-II, q. 42, a. 2, ad 3; q. 104, a. 6, ad 3), as accepted by prominent Spanish theologians such as Domingo Báñez (1594, *De Iure et Iustitia*, q. 44, a. 3), Juan Mariana (1599, *De rege et regis institutione*), and Francisco Suárez (1613, *Defensio Fidei*, VI, iv, 15), even after the Council of Constance (1415) condemned tyrannicide.

Illustration by Teodoro de Bry for Girolamo Benzoni, *La Historia del Mondo Nuovo* (1594). Photo by Carlos A. Jáuregui.

In many of his writings, Las Casas both contemplated and justified the resistance of the Indians to colonial tyranny. However, his was more a cautionary admonition to the empire, a compelling reason for implementing the remedies he outlined, than an explicit call for insurrection. In a letter to the emperor (1543), Las Casas and his colleague, friar Rodrigo de Adrada, maintained the Indians' right to oppose and surmount their oppressors through "just war against the Christians" on the basis of the unjustified aggressions, homicides, and pillage, which "reduced the Indians to perpetual servitude."[121] In *Tratado de las doce dudas* (Treatise on the Twelve Doubts) (1564), Las Casas insisted that the Indians were entitled to "obstruct and resist" their tormenters,[122] and in *Entre los remedios* (Among the Remedies) (1552), he stated, "the prince must remove from power

121. Las Casas and Rodrigo de Adrada, "Memorial al emperador," in *OC*, 13:145.
122. Las Casas, *Tratado de las doce dudas*, in *OC*, 11.2.

he who mistreats or acts as a tyrant with his subjects, and the subjects may . . . even defend themselves with weapons. Because whosoever misuses the power to govern does not deserve to rule; and nobody is obliged to trust or obey the tyrant or accept his law."[123] In *Complaint of the Indians,* insurrection surfaces at one point as the remedy of choice for the Indians, but by the end of the first part of the play, the character designated "Other Indian" finishes the grievance with an appeal that does not have the form or rhetoric of revolt or even passive resistance, but does have the unmistakable flavor of litigation. He proposes a Lascasian request for legal imperial remedies (against tyranny), and also a subsidiary juridical *petitum:* if a sentence against the power of the tyrant encomendero remains unfeasible, then the complainants beg the court to provide for their own merciful extermination: "And if there's no remedy here, / Let us live not one more day, / . . . Better carry us away / And free us from such tyranny" (316–20). Death itself becomes the sole means of liberation from tyrannical oppression and exploitation (a "remedy" that attacks the illness by killing the patient). Until that end arrives, they must endure all the injustices. As previously noted, Death commiserates with the presuppositions of the Indians' grievance—"Oh, how very right you are, / My brothers, to complain" (321–22)—but does not rule in opposition to the wars, the exploitation of labor, or the plundering of the Indies. She does not "wrest away the control" from the colonial "beasts of prey"; instead, she glosses the scriptures and informs the Indians that their pains through injustice are required for redemption,[124] and then proceeds to counsel patience and sustained faith in God (326–50). Hence,

123. "El señor que trata mal o tiránicamente a sus súbditos, se le debe quitar la jurisdicción por el príncipe, y los subditos . . . [pueden] aún defenderse dél con armas. Porque el que usa mal del dominio no es digno de señorear, y al tirano ninguna fe, obediencia ni ley se le debe guardar" (Las Casas, *Entre los remedios,* 759–60).

124. The thesis of necessary penitence has its basis in the declaration of Christ that suffering is in general necessary, particularly that of his own for the salvation of mankind. The verses paraphrase the Bible: "Woe unto the world because of offences! for it must needs be that offences come; but woe to that man by whom the offence cometh!" (Matthew 18:7); "And ye shall hear of wars and rumours of wars: see that ye be not troubled: for all these things must come to pass, but the end is not yet" (Matthew 24:6); "The Son of man must suffer many things, and be rejected of the elders and chief priests and scribes, and be slain, and be raised the third day" (Luke 9:22); etc.

Death does not endorse rebellion, although she does allude to some mode of resistance:

> Believe nothing that they say,
> Beware, that they're a pestilence
> For the soul, and they would bind it
> And force it to eternal torment
> Unless some resistance they find.
> (346–50)

What kind of resistance is this? More akin to religious defiance than to a violent political rebellion, the stated revolt against tyrants resides in the realm of conscience: "Believe nothing that they say." In other words, instead of deposing these tyrants, merely distrust them!

Death's remedy defers justice to the afterlife. In this sense, the work coincides with history itself, and in particular with the equivocal outcome of the historic dispute between Las Casas and Sepúlveda in Valladolid. The debate's failure to produce clear resolutions or effective policies casts the shadow of moral doubt over colonialism, but it does not impede its continuation. In *Complaint of the Indians*, something similar occurs in the eschatological postponement of justice that Death proposes and the saints maintain. Saint Augustine paraphrases the Bible as he solicits the necessary continuation of Indian labor; now is the "time for working" (353), until the night comes "when no man can work" (355). When that will be, the saint does not say, noting only that time flies, so at least they will not have to wait forever (351–60). This advice of patience, of course, translates to the mandate to keep working. In a similar order of ideas (predestination, resignation), Saint Dominic prescribes listening to the divine word: "Listen always, my beloved, / To the word of God Almighty, / The most royal of all *medicines*" (361–63; emphasis added). Here the English translation "medicines" does not reproduce the irregular spelling and variant pronunciation of the Spanish "midecina." This spelling is inconsistent with that which appears in line 146 (the Parthian's "medicina" against Crassus), but there is more here than a simple spelling discrepancy. Here, "medicina" and "midecina" are in fact two signifiers semantically and politically antithetical to one another. In *Complaint of the Indians,* the indigenous "medicina" (like that of the Parthians) is insurrection in the face of tyranny—making the conquistadors swallow molten gold—whereas the royal "midecina"[125] of the second part means the "divine word," invariable patience, and a Christian tolerance for their tortures. Saint Francis seconds Saint Dominic and observes that the Indians are already drinking from "the heavenly fountains," making reference to Christ as the divine fountain, the absolute medicine for all suffering and need (John 4:14). The *pharmakon,*[126] signifier of resistance against colonial appetite, reverts into a recipe for resignation and submissive obedience: the Indians are supposed to swallow the abuses of tyranny. "Medicina" thus becomes something different than itself: a palliative "midecina." Spelling inconsistencies were quite common in the sixteenth century; the point here is that the metathesis of the two first vowels, deliberate or not, marks the cancellation of the political theory of resistance to tyranny and of the very essence of Lascasian thought: justice on earth. What was Las Casas's position regarding the medicine of insurrection vis-à-vis the "midecina" of resignation dispensed from the "heavenly fountains" of the Christian word? In his "Memorial sumario a Felipe II" (1556), he warns that Christian doctrine is insufficient to avert rebellions: "Would they be so religious and humble as to endure this with patience, as penitence, and for the love of Jesus Christ? Is it not quite obvious that they will wake up, revolt, and kill the *encomenderos* and even disobey the viceroy and the *Audiencia* (of your Majesty), and generate a thousand disorders, especially since they do not have anything to eat and have served your Majesty against those traitors [who rose up] against your highness."[127]

125. "Midecina real" could be also translated as "real medicine."
126. See an extended discussion of the *différance* within the *pharmakon* (from poison to remedy) in Derrida's *Dissemination.* Derrida's discussion pertains to his reading of Plato's *Phaedrus,* and of writing itself, and leads to his deconstruction of *phonocentrism.* Still, his very suggestive observation of the instability of the *pharmakon* allows me to extrapolate his analyses for a reading of the two metaphorical uses of the word medicine in this play (for insurrection and for submission).
127. "¿Serán tan religiosos y modestos que lo reciban en paciencia y penitencia por amor de Jesucristo? ¿No está claro que habrán de despertar y amotinarse y matar a los encomenderos y aun desacatar al visorrey y Audiencia de su Majestad y hacer mill bullicios, mayormente que los que mas no tienen que comer y han contra los traidores a Vuestra Malestar servido?" (Las Casas, "Memorial sumario a Felipe II," 312).

In other words, if the Spanish, Christian encomenderos disobeyed and resisted the Crown, as they did after the New Laws, under the pretext of unjust causes (to keep their encomiendas), why should the Indians (whose cause was legitimate) not rise up against these tyrants? While always considering the option of insurrection, Las Casas certainly preferred intervention by the state. Most of his memorials to the Council of the Indies, Charles V, and Philip II were, as previously stated, requests for imperial remedies and justice within the institutional political frame of the empire. However, as Las Casas acknowledged, the empire never gave "any other remedy to all these wrongs than patches here and there."[128] The Lascasian "medicine" is an appeal for true remedy, while the character of the Saint Dominic "midecina" calls for a conformation to colonial cruelties; a spiritual patch, so to speak. It looks like medicina or remedy, but it is actually, on the contrary, a poison that perpetuates the illness. Las Casas was justly concerned that "those proposing a remedy to the Indies" were in fact "gold-plating and disguising the poison of tyranny."[129]

Complaint of the Indians presents a Lascasian defense of the Indians and a fervent accusation against conquerors and encomenderos, and it criticizes the colonial appetite for metals. But then it asks for patience and faith in a supernatural and ahistorical vision of divine retribution. The medicine-justice defers to the midecine-submission of Christian eschatology. This anti-Lascasian aspect of Carvajal's work—"disguising the poison of tyranny"—intensifies toward the play's conclusion, when Saint Dominic, the principal "Lascasian" character, relocates his criticisms to the Indies and their gold:

> O Indies, why did you show
> Europe these treacherous metals
> That drew her with their false lure,
> Only to send her back home
> Loaded with so many evils?
> Didn't she already have mines

128. Las Casas, "Carta al maestro fray Bartolomé Carranza," 280.
129. "Todos los que hablan de medios en esta materia, no pretenden poner remedio en las Yndias, sino fucar y dorar o encubrir el veneno de la tiranía" (ibid., 281).

Abundant mines didn't she hold,
Rich enough and deep with sins,
Without you piling on top
The thorns of a daily death?

O Indies, who opened the door
To these miserable mortals
Only to bring brawling and sorrow!
Indies, who hold wide open
The very jaws of damnation,
Indies, abyss of sinfulness,
Indies, wealthy with evil,
Indies, home for unfortunates,
Indies, that with gold pieces
Paved the pathways of sin!

                    (391–410)

Saint Dominic transfers blame from the Spaniards' avarice for
metals to the seductive nature of the New World. The martyrdom
that he depicts is not that of the Indian or the Indies but of Europe!
For the saint, the New World tortures Europe with the "thorns"
of sin. In a discursive turn—unimaginable to Las Casas—Saint
Dominic seeks and "finds" the drowned upriver: he blames the
"Indies, abyss of sinfulness," for introducing the "treacherous metals" that corrupted Europe (391–410). The Lascasian representation
of America—characterized by the conquest, slavery, despoilment,
death, and violence of what Marx, in eminently material terms,
would call "primitive accumulation"—is replaced here by the spuri-
ous and "suffering" body of Spain, tainted and even "martyred"
by American riches. Through this inversion, the countercolonial
critiques that the play had expressed turn out to be, in fact, "gold-
plating and disguising the poison of tyranny."

    Satan, Flesh, and World have the last word in Carvajal's *Com-
plaint of the Indians*. These conceptual characterizations of the conquistadors, distanced from their evangelical and spiritual "duties,"
insist upon material motives for the conquest of the New World
rather than the spiritual ones of their counterparts, the saints. Satan,
representative of the development of protocapitalist desire (in contrast to the evangelical self-definition of the empire), excuses the

exploitation of the Indies for material gain by invoking the "powerful magnet" of gold (411–20). Flesh points out how the impoverished peoples of Europe must travel to America "searching / For something to eat and to wear" in order to avoid hunger (421–30); moreover—in a comic twist—he ascribes the blame to women (431–40). World, for his part, refers to the freedom and pleasures that individuals seek and satisfy in the New World (441–50).

The critique of coloniality from within is plagued by implacable moral ambushes and is often bound up in the same logic of injustice that it tries to combat. This colonial functionality of countercolonial discourse may explain why colonialism can and does often breed its own critique. Deference to reactionary disenchantments and naïve utopias aside, it must be recognized that, more often than we would like—in the middle of the sixteenth century as well as in the present—countercolonial thought is not a loose wheel but rather a well-oiled gear of the machinery of colonialism. Thought that rubs against the grain of colonialism frequently collaborates—despite itself—to bring grist to the mill of imperial reason. In *Complaint of the Indians,* Las Casas becomes a specter of himself as his discourse is conjured up and translated into the ideology of empire. But, as Derrida reminds us, never is a specter more pertinent than in that moment when, through that equivocal act of conjuring (that is, conjuring as an exorcism, confabulation, and invocation), it reappears, protests, and announces the possibility of justice-to-come.[130]

The play might be read as a dramatic attempt to symbolically conjure colonial anxieties over the resistance, insurrections, and endless defiance of colonial domination. In other words, the replacement of the indigenous medicine-insurrection with medicine-resignation is a symbolic figuration of political desire, but always more than an imperialist fantasy of colonial submission; by deferring justice, the call for resignation announces itself as a nonsolution, a palliative and even a poison rather than a cure. Moreover, by marking the *différance* between "medicina" and "midecina," between insurrection and submission, the play reiterates the indefinite continuous present of injustice and, thus, the radical openness of the future. The

---

130. Jacques Derrida, *Specters of Marx: The State of the Debt, the Work of Mourning, and the New International,* trans. Peggy Camuf (New York: Routledge, 1994).

"remedio" that perpetuates injustice also triggers the ever-present threat of rebellion.

Imperialism in the play, as well as in history, may seem to have spoken the last word. But this ending is not the end of it, for renewed forms of colonialism continue and are at the same time repeatedly contested throughout the present, despite the eschatological postponement of justice that the specious triumph of the "midecina" of resignation and subjugation seems to indicate. Las Casas understood this well when, at the end of his life, he wrote to the Council of the Indies: "We have illegally usurped all the kingdoms of the Indies.... The people from all those lands ... have the right, which will be theirs till the Day of Judgment, to make just war against us and erase us from the face of the earth."[131] In other words, he signaled toward a *remedio* outside the courts and the hands of the empire, a remedy beyond his own relentless legalistic efforts and his own obstinate ethical and political bet on justice.

Complaint of the Indians is an ambiguous colonial epilogue to Lascasianism: the play, while it calls attention to the compelling problem of the extraordinary violence of early colonialism in the New World, still justifies imperial designs. Moreover, and most precisely, it longs for the colonized to accept their subordinated position and abandon any pretensions of justice here on earth; it summons Las Casas in order to exorcise the all-pervading threat of insurrection that he had the courage to name. Yet this subordination to empire was not—and still is not—a settled and unequivocal matter. At the very moment of being exorcised, the specter of countercolonial resistance returns.

---

131. "Todos los reinos y señoríos de las Indias tenemos usurpados.... Las gentes naturales de todas las partes y cualesquiera dellas donde hemos entrado en las Indias, tienen el derecho adquirido de hacernos guerra justísima y raernos de la faz de la tierra, y este derecho les durará hasta el día del juicio." Las Casas, "Memorial de Fray Bartolomé de las Casas al Consejo de Indias," in *De regia potestate o derecho de autodeterminación,* ed. Luciano Pereña (Madrid: Consejo Superior de Investigaciones Científicas, 1969), 282–83.

Note on the Translation

Translation is the result of dialogic and analytical reading and creative writing. That has indeed been the method followed here: this work is a collaborative endeavor made up of multiple instances of (re)reading, discussion, and debate. The process started with a critical reading of a text written in the sixteenth century in Spanish. An initial determination of meaning, or interpretation, was necessary, as well as an understanding of the situation of this text in its literary and historical contexts (see introduction). The translation from the original Spanish into English constituted, then, the translation of a reading, and therefore, in truth, the translation of a translation.

We tried to balance academic concerns with poetic creation, which involved continuous discussions and negotiations of meaning, as well as the assistance of many colleagues and friends. On countless occasions, the translating task made us return to the original to reread and reinterpret lines that had seemed clear in Spanish until they were to be rendered into English. Then, too, the play sometimes showed a resilient semantic resistance to interpretation. Translation became an arduous mano a mano with undecidability, uncertainty, and the dissemination of meaning, and ultimately with the creative task of the reader-translator.

Translation creates a radical linguistic defamiliarization that forces us to recognize the *Unheimlich* within the familiar text. The result is in itself both familiar and strange, the already supplementary outcome of a "perfidious fidelity." The stubborn determination to be true to the text is inseparable from the fate of producing in each translated line a difference—a difference always inviting the possibility of alternative versions. In fact, every fresh reading of a translation we deemed final second-guessed its "finality" and prompted, time and again, new corrections and changes. We have learned that to translate is also to abandon. Thus, we leave *Complaint of the Indians in the Court of Death* to the readers, students, and critics who will make renewed sense of it. In this same spirit, we offer them, alongside the annotated English translation, a parallel Spanish text and, at the end, as an appendix, a facsimile of the 1557 edition of the play. The Spanish text offered here regularizes most of the spelling[1] and adds punctuation to the 1557 published text. This presentation offers readers a wider textuality that we hope will contribute to its study.

Carvajal was a talented and educated writer concerned with rhythm and rhyme, careful in his lexical choices and possessing a refined sense of the language. At the same time, *Cortes de la Muerte* is not a pedantic play; its hyperbatons are used with discretion and its tropes are accessible to the common reader. Carvajal's versification, as noted by Gillet, is "skillful and unusually smooth."[2] He composed *Cortes de la Muerte* in octosyllabic double quintillas, with few metric irregularities and with traditional rhymes.

In the interest of remaining as faithful as possible to both the spirit and the letter of the original, we decided to implement a fourfold approach to the translation: (1) to avoid the use of an artificial sixteenth-century literary English language, opting instead for a contemporary register that kept the text readable while maintaining a certain heightening of tone and lexicon, the challenge being to suggest the elegance as well as the directness of Carvajal's diction, whose simplicity is never banal; (2) to maintain, as much as possible, a line-by-line correspondence between the English and Spanish texts; (3) to eschew the regular rhyme scheme and go with a flexible three-beat rhythm, which, together with the somewhat heightened diction and intermittent use of assonance and other musical effects, still retains, we hope, the flavor of poetry; and (4) to provide the reader with alternative translations in footnotes whenever there was compelling reason to do so.

Carlos A. Jáuregui   Mark Smith-Soto

1. The Spanish text corresponds, with some changes and corrections, to the edition published by the Universidad Nacional Autónoma de México in 2002, which I edited. This text retains a few old-fashioned spellings whenever they are required to keep the octosyllabic meter or correspond to the probable pronunciation of the time; for example, *quexarnos* (instead of *quejarnos*), *guiovés* (*genovés*), *midecina* (*medicina*), etc. The assistance of the philologist and linguist Philip D. Rasico has been invaluable in making these decisions.
2. Gillet, introduction to *Tragedia Josephina*, lvii.

Complaint of the Indians in the Court of Death
[Scene XIX of *The Court of Death*], 1557

MICHAEL DE CARVAJAL *and* LUIS HURTADO DE TOLEDO

Translated by CARLOS A. JÁUREGUI *and* MARK SMITH-SOTO

[Fol. 2r, unnumbered] Cortes de la Muerte a las cuales vienen todos los Estados, y por vía de representación, dan aviso a los vivientes y doctrina a los oyentes. Llevan gracioso y delicado estilo. Dirigidas por Luis Hurtado de Toledo al invictísimo señor Don Felipe, Rey de España y Inglaterra, etc., su señor y Rey. Año de MDLvij

———◦◆◦———

Luis Hurtado de Toledo, al serenísimo y muy poderoso señor Don Felipe, Rey de España y Inglaterra, etc., su señor.

Después de haber dedicado, muy alto y muy poderoso Señor, las *Cortes de Casto Amor* a vuestra alteza, hallé por mi cuenta que el vulgo, público examinador de ajenas causas, me había de juzgar por hombre vano, mayormente leyendo el *Espejo de gentileza, Hospitales de damas y galanes,* con otras obras de amor que a vuestra Alteza ofrecí. Y para evitar este daño, pues la buena opinión es joya estimable, y más con el vulgo, determiné también para su enmienda y consideración de ponelles juntamente otras Cortes que hizo la Muerte con todos los Estados, con notable llamamiento, en este año presente; en las cuales, por apacible estilo y delicadas sentencias, cada Estado verá lo que de la Muerte se le puede proveer y en sus Cortes determinar. Las cuales fueron comenzadas por Michael de Carvajal natural de Plasencia, y agradando tal estilo, yo las proseguí y acabé.

Ruego al sumo emperador, por cuya voluntad estas cortes se hacen cada hora, dé a vuestra alteza muchos años de vida contenta y empleada en su servicio. Amen.

[Fol. 2r (unnumbered)]* The Court of Death, to
Which All Estates Come and by Means of
Representatives Warn the Living and Teach
the Audience, in an Elegant and Delicate
Style. Addressed by Luis Hurtado de
Toledo to the Invincible Lord, Don Felipe,
King of Spain and England, etc., Their
Lord and King. In the Year of MDLvij

———◆———

Luis Hurtado de Toledo to the most serene and powerful
lord Don Felipe, King of Spain and England,[1] etc., their Lord.

Having dedicated, most high and powerful Lord, *The Court of
Chaste Love* to your Highness, I realized that commoners examining
matters that are beyond them might judge me to be a frivolous man,

---

* The first foliation (fols. 1r, unnumbered, cover to 42r) includes various works on
the theme of courtly love; the second foliation (fols. 1r, unnumbered, cover, to 68r,
unnumbered) corresponds to *The Court of Death*.

1. This play was published along with six other works in a volume dated
October 15, 1557, and dedicated to the new sovereign, Philip II (1527–98), son of
the Holy Roman Emperor Charles V and Isabella of Portugal. In 1551, Charles V
bequeathed the administration of the Hispanic Kingdoms to Philip, who signed as
Philippus, Hispaniarum Princeps. In 1552, Friar Bartolomé de Las Casas also dedicated his famous *Brevísima relación de la destruición de la Indias* (Brief Account of
the Destruction of the Indies) to Philip II. In 1555, the emperor gave the sovereignty
of the Low Countries to Philip, and in 1556 he abdicated the Spanish crown in favor
of his son. Philip was also king of England from 1554 to 1558, as the husband of the
Catholic Mary I. Charles V saw this union as a step toward overcoming his troubles
in Europe. When Philip was ordered to marry Mary, he had to break the negotiations
for a planned marriage with Mary of Portugal, losing the four hundred thousand
ducats offered as dowry. Philip's economic difficulties were temporarily resolved by
the arrival of a fleet from the Indies with more than three million ducats, nearly half

especially after reading *Mirror of Courtesy, Hospital for Ladies and Gallants,* and other works on courtly love that I have offered to your Majesty.[2] And so to avoid this moral harm, since a proper insight is a jewel to be esteemed, above all in the case of the common people, I determined, in order to improve and instruct them, to offer them also this other court that Death held with all estates,[3] after a general convocation, in this current year;[4] in which, with a gentle style and

---

a million of which went directly to the imperial purse. The colonial treasure from the New World footed the bill for Philips's extravagant trip to England in 1554 for the wedding, accompanied by his court (nearly three thousand people) and his army (more than six thousand soldiers). By the terms of the marriage contract, Philip was the consort of the queen and not a ruler of England, but from the beginning the Spanish Crown had high hopes for Spanish influence. Mary was attracted to Philip (who was eleven years her junior), and he was able to influence English international policy. By 1557—when the *Court of Death* used the title "king of England"—Philip (during his second and last visit to England) was able to obtain some support from the English. He left England in July of 1557 to wage war against France and the pope, who threatened to excommunicate him. Again, the apparently inexhaustible wealth of the West Indies came to the rescue of the Spanish Empire, providing the necessary funds (two million ducats) for the war in Italy and Flanders. Mary died in 1558 without an heir, dashing the promise of this alliance masterminded by Charles V.

2. Hurtado de Toledo is referring to other "light" compositions included in the same volume with *The Court of Death,* such as *Cortes de casto amor hecha en la floreciente ribera del Tajo en los reales Palacios del marítimo bosque* [fols. 4v–10r]; *Hospital de galanes enamorados compuesto por uno que en él ya hace* [yace] *con mayor enfermedad y menos remedio, a la fin salud espera* [fols. 25r–31r]; *Hospital de damas de amor heridas compuesto por una dellas; hermosa, sabia y graciosa, aunque por ello más llagada* [fols. 31v–38r]; y *Espejo de gentileza para damas y galanes cortesanos compuesto por el Toledano autor, que hizo los Espitales de Amor* [fols. 38r–44v] (The Court of Chaste Love on the Flowering Bank of the Tajo River in the Royal Palaces of the Maritime Forest; Hospital for Love-Struck Young Gallants Composed by One Who Already Lies There with a Greater Illness and Less of a Cure, [whereas] in the End He Awaits Health; Hospital for Ladies Wounded by Love, by One of the Same: Beautiful, Wise and Witty, Although for Those Reasons all the More Injured; and Mirror of Courtesy for Ladies and Gentlemen by the Author from Toledo, Who Wrote the Hospitals of Love). Hurtado de Toledo's "moral disclaimer"—conventionally, perhaps—indicates that the work has a moral and pedagogical intention: the seriousness of *The Court of Death* offers a balance to the general wittiness of the volume illustrated by the titles of the other works.

3. Sp. "todos los estados." The "estados del reino" "are the three Arms of the kingdom, as they are called, that have a vote in the *Cortes,* and are convened for serious matters: the first is the ecclesiastical arm, formed by prelates and dignitaries of the Church; the second is formed by grandees and noblemen; and the third by the cities that have this privilege" (RAE, *Autoridades* 1732, 623).

4. "Cortes," always in plural in Spanish but translated here as "court," seems to refer to two kinds of institutions: (1) a tribunal in which juridical cases are heard and resolved; and (2) the representative assembly of the states of the kingdom—nobility,

delicate admonitions, each estate will see what it can expect from Death and what judgments from its court. This work was begun by Michael de Carvajal, native of Plasencia, and I, in admiration of its style, did continue and complete it.[5]

I pray to the highest of emperors,[6] by whose will this court is at all times in session, that your Highness may enjoy many years of a happy life devoted to his service. Amen.

<hr />

clergy, and towns (the people or commoners)—something of an advisory council formed by royal convocation to pronounce on important political issues. In general terms, "Cortes" refers to "the meeting and session of the representatives of the cities and villages that have voting privileges, in order to propose and declare what is in the interest of the king and the kingdom" (RAE, *Autoridades* 1729, 628). "In Castile the *Cortes* are the session of the three estates of the kingdom that the king summons to take advice from his subjects in difficult cases and important business. The *Cortes* are formed by the three arms, the Church, the nobility, and the people. Archbishops and bishops, headed by the archbishop of Toledo, form the ecclesiastic arm; the nobility is comprised of the grandees, lords, and some noblemen whose families enjoy this privilege. The estate of the people or commoners is represented by representatives or delegates from the kingdoms, cities, and villages that have the privilege to vote in the *Cortes*. . . . The arm of the representatives of the kingdoms expresses the burdens and wrongs that the towns and provinces suffer and calls for their remedy." RAE, *Diccionario de la lengua castellana* (Madrid: Joaquín Ibarra, 1780), 284. In using the word "court," the play seems to take advantage of both its possible meanings, staging a series of complaints before a judge (Death) and an allegorical assembly where different and heterogeneous sectors of society come before the ultimate terrestrial sovereign, which is, again, Death. The reference to a "general convocation, in this current year" might seem to be related to either the Cortes de Valladolid (1555), called by Doña Juana in the name of the emperor, or the Cortes de Madrid (1551–52), celebrated around the same time as the Junta de Valladolid and the famous debate between Las Casas and Ginés de Sepulveda. The Cortes in the play are of course an allegorical or conceptual scenario, related to the medieval tradition of the Dance of Death (see introduction).

5. The play was written by Carvajal (for a discussion on Hurtado de Toledo's intervention, please see the introduction, section 2).

6. Sp. "Ruego al sumo emperador," meaning "I pray to God."

[Fol. 51r] ESCENA XIX

INTERLOCUTORES:

Cacique Indio
Muerte
San Agustín
San Francisco
Santo Domingo
Satanás
Carne
Mundo

Tañen las trompetas, y entran los indios:

CACIQUE   ¶ Los indios ocidentales
y estos caciques venimos

[Fol. 51r] SCENE XIX[7]

INTERLOCUTORS:

Chieftain
Death
Saint Augustine
Saint Francis
Saint Dominic
Satan
Flesh
World
Another Indian and Another [Indian or
Chieftain] [characters not announced in
the original text][8]

The trumpets sound and the Indians enter:

CHIEFTAIN   We Indians from Occident
And we chieftains here have come

---

7. Fols. 51r–53v. Scene XIX has a total of 450 lines, though one of them (line 16) is missing. The first 320 lines correspond to the intervention of the Indians and the remaining 130 to the dramatic speeches of Death, the saints, and Satan, Flesh, and World.

8. Various Indian characters participate in the play, though not all of them are announced at the beginning of the scene. There are eleven interventions by Indian characters, in the following order: 1. Chieftain (announced) (1–120); 2. Another Indian (121–40); 3. Chieftain (announced or another) (141–65); 4. Another (Indian or chieftain) (166–80); 5. Chieftain (announced or another) (181–210); 6. Chieftain (most likely different than the preceding character) (211–40); 7. Another Indian (241–60); 8. Chieftain (announced or another) (261–80); 9. Another Indian (281–300); 10. Chieftain (announced or another) (301–10); and 11. Another Indian (311–20). The chieftain says "We Indians" and "we chieftains" at the beginning of the scene (lines 1 and 2), which indicates that several Indian characters, and certainly more than one chieftain, are coming to complain in the Court of Death. Although there is only one chieftain announced at the beginning of the scene, it is possible that two or up to four different characters—all called chieftain—participate in the scene. The two chieftains who speak one after another (181–210 and 211–40) are certainly different characters. We must assume that there are at least two and maybe up to five Indian characters besides the two chieftains. All of these characters speak and present their case in lines 1–320; thereafter, for the remaining 130 lines, they remain silent and listen to the other characters, including Death and the saints.

a tus Cortes triunfales
a quexarnos de los males
y agravios que recibimos.   5
Que en el mundo no tenemos
rey ni roque que eche aparte
las rabias que padecemos;
y por lo tanto a ti queremos,
Muerte, dar quexas del arte.   10

¶ Pues tú sola, ques razón,
sabrás que siendo paganos
y hijos de perdición,
por sola predicación
venimos a ser cristianos;   15
. . . .
como habrás oído y visto,
seguimos ya la doctrina
y la escuela y disciplina
del maestro Jesu Cristo   20

To this, your triumphal court,[9]
To air grievance of the harm
And injuries we have borne.   5
For in all the world we can find
No king or champion to help us[10]
With the outrages we suffer;
Which is why we wish to make
Our complaint to you, O Death.   10

Naturally, you must know
That when we were nothing but pagans,[11]
Just children lost on our way,
By the simple path of the Word
We found our way to the Lord;   15
. . . . [12]
As you must have seen and heard,
We do now follow the teachings,
The philosophy and way
Of our master, Jesus Christ   20

9. In Scene XIX, the estate that comes to present its case to the Cortes presided over by Death is comprised of Indians "from Occident." "Occidentales" means from the Indies or from the New World, America, otherwise called Occident. Although the play does not say explicitly where this Court is being held, the assembly/court appears to be in Spain, since the Indies are referred to as "over there" ("allá") throughout the text (i.e., lines 70, 93, 164, 166, 241, 258, 286, 296, 376, 427), and the Indians say that they "have come" ("venimos") from the Occident (that is, from the New World) to the Cortes situated "over here" ("acá"), the center of the empire.

10. Sp. "no tenemos / rey ni roque que eche aparte / las rabias que padecemos"— literally, "we have / neither king nor castle able / to keep at bay the pains we suffer." "Ni rey ni roque" is an expression that excludes everyone; it is the same as saying "nobody," or in context: "we have nobody who can help us."

11. For Las Casas—as well as for these Lascasian Indians—the distinction between categories of unbelievers, especially pagans and heretics, is very important. Heretics, unlike pagans, fell under the jurisdiction of the Crown and the Church, and therefore they could justly be subdued by force. Pagans were considered "outside the law" and external to the Church.

12. The play is organized into stanzas of ten lines, each stanza invariably marked (see facsimile). The second stanza here has only nine lines; this irregularity indicates that either the printer or Luis de Toledo mistakenly omitted a line. The rhyme scheme, abaab cdccd, makes it clear that the missing line in stanza 2 is line 16: abaab [c]dccd.

¶ y estamos ya tan ufanos
con la merced singular
de habernos vuelto cristianos,
que a los altos soberanos
no vemos con qué pagar.   25
Mas ¿qué casos son tan crudos?
tú, Muerte, nos da a entender;
que cuando a los dioses mudos,
bestiales, falsos y rudos
adorábamos sin ser,   30

¶ ninguno nos perturbaba
de cuantos en nuestra tierras
ha pasado ni pasaba,
ni mataba, ni robaba
ni hacía crudas guerras;   35
y agora que ya, cuitados,
nos habíamos de ver
un poco más regalados,
por sólo tener los grados
de cristiandad en tal ser,   40

¶ parece que desafueros,
homicidios, fuegos, brasas,
casos atroces y fieros,
por estos negros dineros
nos llueven en nuestras casas.   45
¡Oh, Dios! ¿y qué adversidades
son estas? ¿No entendéis esto?

And we are, in fact, so proud
Of the most singular blessing
Of being taken to Christ
That we feel helpless to repay
The royal sovereigns the favor.[13]   25
But what fate could be so cruel,
Tell us, O Death, as we've suffered;
Given that, before we were Christians
And still worshipped the silent gods,[14]

Crude, bestial, and false,   30
Of the men who year after year
Traveled throughout our lands,
Not one disturbed us at all,
Not one came to kill or rob us,
Or wage cruel warfare upon us.   35
And now that we've seen the light
And should by all rights enjoy
Even a more pleasant life
As the reward justly due
To those whose life is now pious,   40

It seems that, wretched, instead
We get injustice, murder, and fire,
Fierce and terrible events
Brought down upon our heads
By that cursed wealth within our land.   45
Dearest Heaven, what kind of misfortune
Is this? How do you explain it?[15]

13. The Indians of the Cortes have already converted to Christianity, making
their mistreatment all the more unjust and paradoxical.

14. "Silent gods": that is, idols, or false gods that do not speak to men; that do
not impart the Word. This trope, like many others in the play, paraphrases the Bible:
"Ye know that ye were Gentiles, carried away unto these dumb idols, even as ye were
led" (1 Corinthians 12:2). In Psalms there is another reference to mute idols: "Their
idols are silver and gold, the work of men's hands. They have mouths, but they speak
not" (Psalms 115:4–5; see also Revelation 9:20).

15. Here, the Indian chieftain is apparently addressing Death, not God, as
in the preceding line. The same happens after line 50. These are rhetorical and

¡Pagar con mil crueldades
todas las necesidades
del mundo! Di: ¿Qué es aquesto?   50

[Fol. 51v] ¶ ¿Cómo estamos obligados
que todo género humano
enriquezcamos, cuitados;
y tras eso, aperreados
y muertos de ajena mano?   55
¿No nos basta proveer
las miserias de parientes,
las de hijos y mujer,
sino haber de sostener
las de todas esas gentes?   60

¶ ¿Quién nunca vido al inglés,
ni al húngaro, ques de porte,
ni al bohemio, ni al francés,
ni español, ni ginovés
debaxo de otro norte?   65
Por ventura ¿han acabado
todo el mundo despojar
que cosa no haya quedado,
pues, que con tanto cuidado
nos vayan allá a buscar?   70

¶ Y ¿Cómo aquellas riquezas
de aquella felice Arabia,
Tarsis, Sabá y sus grandezas

To pay with a thousand sorrows
For the pressing needs and wants
Of the world! Tell us, what's this?   50

[Fol. 51v] Why are we so obliged
To enrich at our own expense
All other humankind,
Only to be then struck down
Like dogs by a stranger's hand?[16]   55
Is it not enough we provide
For the needs of our own blood,
Those of our children and wives,
Without having to bear as well
The burdens of all these peoples?   60

Who hasn't seen the English
And the proper Hungarians as well,
The Bohemians and the French,
The Spaniards and the Genoese,[17]
All follow the same North Star?   65
Have they, by any chance, finished
Exploiting the rest of the world
Until nothing's been left behind,
That now they pour so much effort
In rooting around our lands?   70

And, what? How is it that neither
The wealth of most prosperous Araby
Nor the riches of Sheba or Tharshish[18]

---

argumentative questions: for the Indians there is no justifiable explanation for the
colonial cruelty, violence, and plundering.

16. The adjective "aperreado" in the Spanish original also means "exhausted,
tired, beaten" (RAE, *Autoridades* 1726, 336); an alternative translation for lines 54–55
would be "Only then to be beaten / and slaughtered by strangers."

17. In the middle of the sixteenth century, "Genoese" included people not only
from Genoa, but also from the Italian peninsula and Flanders.

18. Sheba: a city of pre-Islamic Arabia, proverbial for its riches, mentioned frequently in the Bible: "And when the queen of Sheba heard of the fame of Solomon,

no han hartado las bravezas
de aquesta rabiosa rabia? 75
Los rubíes rutilantes
de Narsinga tan reales,
los zafires y diamantes
no han bastado a estos gigantes,
sin buscar nuestros metales. 80

¶ Pues ¡mezquinos! ¿a dó iremos
huyendo del mal gobierno

Have sufficed to quiet the hunger[19]
Of such insatiable avarice? 75
All the radiant, fiery rubies
From the kingdom of Narsinga,[20]
All its sapphires and its diamonds,
Have not kept these famished giants[21]
From wanting to glut on our metals. 80

But where can we go, poor wretches,
To escape such unjust governing[22]

---

she came to prove Solomon with hard questions at Jerusalem, with a very great company, and camels that bare spices, and gold in abundance, and precious stones: and when she was come to Solomon, she communed with him of all that was in her heart" (2 Chronicles 9:1). Tharshish, Tarshish, or Tharsis: a biblical city known for its riches (silver, in particular): "For the king [Solomon] had at sea a navy of Tharshish with the navy of Hiram: once in three years came the navy of Tharshish, bringing gold, and silver, ivory, and apes, and peacocks" (1 Kings 10:22).

19. Sp. "aquella rabiosa rabia," literally "that ferocious [thirst of] rabies." Rabies is associated here with the hunger and thirst of dogs. The Spanish verb "rabiar" "metaphorically, means to crave and to desire something, eagerly and with extreme fervor" (RAE, *Autoridades* 1737, 478). See also notes to lines 55, 148, and 243.

20. This is an allusion to the Portuguese colonial adventures in India. Narsinga was one of the names used by Europeans (particularly Portuguese explorers and merchants) for Vijayanagar or Bisnagar, the last powerful Hindu kingdom and greatest empire of southern India, destroyed in 1614. Narsinga, legendary for its opulence, riches, and precious stones, was a common cartographic reference during the Renaissance. Joan Pau Rubiés, *Travel and Ethnology in the Renaissance: South India Through European Eyes, 1250–1625* (Cambridge: Cambridge University Press, 2000), 11. Renowned Portuguese poet Luis de Camões mentions the opulence of the kingdom of Narsinga in his *Os Lusíadas:* "O Reino de Narsinga, poderoso / Mais de ouro e pedras que de forte gente" (canto 7, st. 21) [The powerful kingdom of Narsinga / Richer in gems and gold than soldiers]. Luís de Camões, *The Lusíads*, trans. Landeg White (Oxford: Oxford University Press, 1997), 143.

21. The conquistadors and the encomenderos are possessed by a horrendous and teratological greed—hence the allusion to the giants. This constitutes a remarkable inversion of the notion of American monstrosity. According to the Indian in *The Court of Death*, the conquistadors are the insatiable "giants" of the teratological traditions of Antiquity and the Middle Ages.

22. Sp. "Mal gobierno," unjust or ill government, is a key legal and political concept related to the right of resistance or rebellion against tyranny as well as to the concept of *remedios del reino* or proposals of corrective measures for a just and effective government. Las Casas portrays the agents of empire (not the empire itself) as tyrants by both usurpation and oppression. This implies, on the one hand, the right of the Indian subjects (as Christians and members of the empire) to resist tyrants and, on the other, the obligation of the sovereign to relieve his subjects from oppression.

que más gente no enviemos
si a nuestra ley nos volvemos
a las penas del infierno?   85
¡Oh hambre pestilencial
la de aqueste oro maldito
y desta gente bestial
hacen tamaño caudal
de tan malvado apetito!   90

¶ Una cosa que les damos
de buena gana y en paz,
porque allá no lo estimamos

Without falling back on old ways
That would condemn all our peoples
To the just punishments of Hell?[23]   85
Oh, what a sick hungering
For this damnation called gold[24]
Impels these bestial people
To make such a lavish fortune
From such an appetite for evil!   90

And this for something we'd gladly
Hand over to them in peace,
Because we don't prize it back home[25]

In most of Las Casas's writings, references to good and ill government and tyranny are indeed about the responsibility or obligation of the state and the need for the empire to intervene and impart justice. Nevertheless, in principle, an unbearable *mal gobierno* or tyranny, without *remedio*, justifies rebellion. Note that so far the Indian characters of this play are talking about escaping the unjust government rather than opposing it or overthrowing it. Compare this with the Indian's proposal in lines 141–50 and with line 350 (see introduction, Section 5).

23. In other words, how to escape the unjust colonial oppression without abandoning Christianity; recall that the chieftain has already expressed his gratitude to the royal sovereigns for the favor of "being taken to Christ" (24–25).

24. In 1550 and 1551, silver and gold imports from the Indies nearly doubled from the previous decade; 303,121 kg of silver and 42,000 kg of gold arrived in Spain from the New World. Silver imports would reach 2,707,626 kg in the last decade of the sixteenth century ("the cycle of silver"). The decade of gold, however, was 1551–60; during no other moment did Spain obtain so much gold from the Indies as during this ten-year period (Le Flem, "Los aspectos económicos de la España moderna," 70).

25. This ignorance regarding the exchange value of gold corresponds to a stereotypic ethnographic notion of the New World's economy as primitive and prior to property, greed, and the use of money, and therefore free from the despicable appetite for gold. Pedro Mártir de Anglería (1457–1526), for example, applauds the indigenous people for their system of communal property, for not knowing the significance of "the words 'yours' and 'mine,'" *seed of all evil*," and for living "in a plentiful golden age" (emphasis added). *Décadas del Nuevo Mundo* (Mexico City: J. Porrúa, 1964), 1:141. The New World often evokes an imaginary reencounter with the mythical golden age of classical Mediterranean antiquity as well as with medieval and Renaissance notions of an idealized savage. The persistent imagining of a New World without work, property, laws, or state paradoxically accompanied the submission and forced exploitation of the labor of hundreds of thousands of human beings, the plundering of metals and raw materials, and the imposition of imperial sovereignty over numerous indigenous peoples. These are the subjects of the Indians' complaint in Carvajal's play. See also lines 281–85 and 291–95.

en tanto, ni reputamos
por causar males asaz.   95
Que aunque la India es tenida
por simple, cierto no yerra
en despreciarlo, y lo olvida;
que al fin es tierra cocida
en las venas de la tierra.   100

¿Qué campos no están regados
con la sangre, que a Dios clama,
de nuestros padres honrados,
hijos, hermanos, criados
por robar hacienda y fama?   105
¿Qué hija, mujer, ni hermana
tenemos que no haya sido
mas que pública mundana

The way they do over here,
Since it causes so much sorrow.   95
And though the Indies be considered
Simple,[26] there can be no mistake
In choosing to spurn and forget
What's really nothing but dirt
Fired in the veins of earth.[27]   100

What fields have now not been fed
With blood crying up to God,
Spilled from our honest parents,
Our sons, our servants, our brothers,
Protecting their homes and their honor?[28]   105
What daughter, sister, or wife
Have we been able to guard
From being used like a whore[29]

26. With similar logic, Las Casas states: "God raised all of these universal and countless peoples *a toto genere* as the most simple [las más simples], without evils or duplicities, very obedient and faithful to their natural masters and to the Christians whom they serve; [they are the] most humble, most patient, most peaceful and calm people, without squabbles, or riots, not lustful, nor quarrelsome, without rancor, without hate, without desiring vengeance" (*Brevísima*, 14). In Spanish, as in English, "simple" and "simplicity" have a wide semantic range, from "fool" to "innocent" and "pure," and from "unsophisticated" to "authentic" and "veritable." The Indians' lack of knowledge of the value of gold makes them innocent; in any case, they have the knowledge of Christ (via conversion). In contrast, the European knowledge of the value of gold makes them idolaters and sinners (see lines 181–85). The Indians will mention again their "lack of ambition" in lines 281–93.

27. The belief that gold, silver, and other metals were like dirt alchemically fired in the veins of the earth had been common since antiquity. The following lines implicitly relate it to the blood from the Indians' veins, suggesting that in order to extract that dirt (gold and silver), the conquistadors must have spilt the blood of the Indians (101–4).

28. This line has been translated with a certain poetic license to keep both the rhythm and the coherence of the stanza. Literally, "por robar hacienda y fama" translates as "for the sake of stealing fortunes and fame" ("fame" as a synonym for good reputation or honor). To steal someone's honor refers here to the raping and sexual abuse of Indian women. So, in context, the Indian is asking: "What place has not been the scene of violence and spilling of Indian blood, all for the sake of stealing fortunes and raping our women?"

29. The motif of honor appears constantly throughout the writings of Las Casas, who accused the conquistadors of raping women and sullying the honor of the indigenous people. In *Del único modo*, Las Casas was appalled by the "evangelical model"

por esta gente tirana
que todo lo ha corrompido?   110

¶ Para sacar los anillos
¿Qué dedos no se cortaron?
¿Qué orejas para zarcillos
no rompieron con cuchillos?
¿Qué brazos no destrozaron?   115
¿Qué vientres no traspasaron
[Fol. 52r] las espadas con gran lloro?
Destos males ¿qué pensaron?
¿Que en los cuerpos sepultaron
nuestros indios su tesoro?   120

OTRO   ¶ ¡Cómo! ¿Por haber venido
INDIO   a la viña del Señor

By these vile and ruthless tyrants
Who corrupt all that they touch?   110

To snatch away golden rings
What fingers did they not sever?
What ears did their knives not slash
For the sake of golden earrings?
What arms did they not break?   115
What wombs, amid cries of woe,
[Fol. 52r] Did they not pierce with their swords?[30]
What were they thinking, doing this?
That our Indians hid their treasure
Within the vessel of their bodies?[31]   120

ANOTHER   What? Is it because we're latecomers
INDIAN   To the vineyards of the Lord,[32]

---

of the rape of women (371), and in the *Brevísima*, he denounced the rapes and sexual
abuses of the sisters and wives of indigenous kings, some of whom were allies of the
Spaniards and subjects of the king. One example was Guarionex, who was "very obedient and virtuous and naturally peaceful, and devoted to the king and queen of Castile" and whose recompense "was to be dishonored by the rape of his wife, by a vile
Christian captain" (*Brevísima*, 26–27). Las Casas also refers to other cases, like that of
Pedro de Alvarado, who in New Spain "robbed the married men by taking their wives
and daughters and giving them to the sailors and soldiers to coax them into carrying
on in their armadas" (ibid., 70–71). He also recounts the case of Nuño de Guzmán,
who, in order to rape a virgin girl, cut off her mother's hand when she tried to defend
her daughter, and finally killed the girl "because she did not want to consent" (75).

   30. Note the commonality with tropes used by Las Casas.

   31. These lines question ironically whether the conquistadors decimated indigenous bodies thinking that wealth was somehow harbored in their interior.

   32. In lines 121–30, the Indian character again argues as a theologian, paraphrasing the Bible: the Indies arrive late to "the vineyards of the Lord" because their
evangelization comes at a later point in history than the European conversion from
paganism. It is a late conversion, yes, but not an inferior one, since the latecomers
to the table of the Lord are nevertheless seated at the same table as the guests who
arrived earlier—and the Bible even suggests the privileged position of the latecomers:
"So when even was come, the lord of the vineyard saith unto his steward, Call the
labourers, and give them their hire, beginning from the last unto the first" (Matthew
20:8). "And they shall come from the east, and from the west, and from the north, and
from the south, and shall sit down in the kingdom of God. And, behold, there are last
which shall be first, and there are first which shall be last" (Luke 13:29–30). So for the
indigenous and recently converted plaintiffs, any temporal difference between new and
old Christians works in favor of the new ones. A Christian egalitarian tradition that

a la tarde, es permitido
que a los que él hubo querido
roben, maten sin temor?   125
Pues ellos han predicado
que tanto dio a los postreros
que en su viña han trabajado,
como a los que han madrugado
y salieron los primeros.   130

¶ ¡Que ley divina ni humana
permita tales molestias,
que una gente ques cristiana,
y que a Dios sirve de gana,
la carguen como a las bestias!   135
¿Quién nunca tal vio, mortales?
me decid que es compasión
que se sirvan de los tales
como de unos animales
brutos y sin más razón.   140

That it's permitted that we,
We, whom He would have loved,
Should be freely robbed and murdered?   125
Why, they themselves have preached
That the last to work in God's fields
Would deserve the same reward
As those who, getting up early,
Arrived first upon the scene.   130

What divine or human law
Would permit such wrongdoing[33]
That a people who embraced Christ
Gladly to serve the Almighty,
Should be bound like beasts of burden?   135
Has any mortal seen such a thing?[34]
Tell me if that is compassion,
That they should treat other people
As if they were nothing but creatures
Dumb and deprived of reason.[35]   140

---

considered all Catholics to be part of the mystic body of the Church resonates in the chrono-theological case presented by the Indian character. It is the same tradition that is embedded within Las Casas's defense of the Indians. There is also a strong echo of the "problem" of the *conversos* and their persecution based on the statutes of "purity of blood" (*pureza de sangre*). This discrimination established—against the New Testament evangelical teleology—an inferior kind of Christians within the Church, based on the temporality of their conversion and that of their parents and grandparents and so on. It is possible, indeed—as some other textual evidence indicates—that this play may be the expression of a peninsular grievance on the behalf of the New Christians through a kind of allegorical ventriloquism: the indianization of the complaints of the *conversos*. In fact, Michael de Carvajal was most likely one of these New Christians (see note 102 in introduction).

33. Note how these lines paraphrase Las Casas: "no human or divine law approves taking the lives of these people, who are naturally peaceful, simple, and good, after taking their properties." "Carta al Consejo de Indias" (1534), in *OC*, 13:83.

34. The syntax of this line in Spanish indicates that the character is addressing the audience: "mortales" means "you mortals," "you people."

35. These lines are making a threefold case: (1) the Indians are not treated with compassion as biblically mandated: "But when He saw the multitudes, he was moved with compassion on them, because they fainted, and were scattered abroad, as sheep having no shepherd" (Matthew 9:36); (2) they are treated as brutes without reason, a common characterization of the indigenous; and (3) they are not brutes, but beings

CACIQUE   ¡Oh, Partos, cuan bien curastes
a Craso, aquel capitán
que por la boca echastes
tanto oro, que matastes
aquella sed y alquitrán!
Desta mesma medicina   145
debiéramos, cierto, usar
con esta hambre canina,

CHIEFTAIN   O Parthians, how well you cured
The rampant fever of Crassus
When down his throat you poured
Enough molten gold to quench
That burning thirst of his![36]
That same medicine is the one   145
We should certainly use[37]
Against that beastlike hunger[38]

---

with reason (what Aristotle called *zôon logistikón*), as recognized by the *Bula Sublimis Deus* 1537, by Paul III: "The enemy of the human race [Satan] . . . invented a means never before heard of, by which he might hinder the preaching of God's word of Salvation to the people: he inspired his satellites who, to please him, have not hesitated to publish abroad that the Indians of the West and the South, and other people of whom We have recent knowledge should be treated as *dumb brutes* created for our service, pretending that they are incapable of receiving the Catholic Faith. . . . The Indians are truly men and they are not only capable of understanding the Catholic Faith but, according to our information, they desire exceedingly to receive it." In Lewis Hanke, "Pope Paul III and the American Indians," *Harvard Theological Review* 30 (1937): 72. It would seem that the Indian characters from *The Court of Death* have read the pope.

    36. Sp. "aquella sed y alquitrán," literally "that thirst and tar," a "metaphorical phrase to characterize the person that is mad and fervent . . . in his desire and craving for something" (RAE, *Autoridades* 1726, 243).

    37. The fate of Marcus Licinius Crassus (115–53 B.C.) is a powerful image of punishment for greed or hunger for metals. This Roman magnate and general, member of the first triumvirate, enriched by the slave trade and exploitation of the mines, was allegedly captured by the Parthians of Persia (53 B.C.) and made to drink liquid gold: "the Parthians, as some say, poured molten gold into his mouth in mockery; for though a man of vast wealth, he had set so great store by money as to pity those who could not support an enrolled legion from their own means, regarding them as poor men" (Cassius Dio 40.27). Dante immortalized this image in his famous lines in canto 20 of *The Divine Comedy*: "Tell us, Crassus, / since you know, what is the taste of gold?" Here the chieftain is calling for an insurrection against the tyrants by evoking the Parthians and Crassus's punishment as examples for the Indians: "That same medicine is the one / We should certainly use" (146–47). Compare this "medicine" with the "royal medicine" proposed by Saint Dominic in line 363.

    38. Sp. "hambre canina," literally "canine hunger." In Spanish, more than in English, the canine trope is predominantly negative and is used to depict abjection, treason, duplicity, sexual promiscuity, irrationality, filth, and religious infidelity. "Dog" and "doglike" are derogatory epithets for Jews, dissolute women, ungrateful subjects, Protestants, etc. (see notes to lines 55 and 74). Furthermore, the Indian characterizes the conquistadors and encomenderos as moral monsters, inverting the stereotypical teratology of cannibals represented as *cynocephali* (dog-heads), an image from the bestiaries and the classical and medieval teratologies that Columbus alludes to (he thought that the "can-" in "cannibal" was etymologically equivalent to "cyno-").

tan fundada en la rapina
y que tanto ha de amargar.   150

¶ ¿Qué locuras son aquestas?
¿Piensa esta gente en el suelo
que del oro hace fiestas,
que ha de ir con la carga a cuestas
como galápago al cielo?   155
Pues tenemos entendido
que si no lo renunciare,
que todo es tiempo perdido,
y perderá lo servido,
si de tal carga cargare.   160

¶ Por ventura como acá
hay tanto y tan gran letrado,
otra cosa alcanzan ya;
pero a nosotros allá
ansí nos lo han predicado.   165

That with its rapacious attacks
So much bitterness must bring.[39]   150

But, what madness is this, then?
Do these revelers really think,
As they pile gold on their backs,
That like Galapagos turtles
They can lug it to heaven with them?[40]   155
Because it's true, as we all know,
That if they don't cast it down
But carry with them that burden,
They are wasting their time and life
And will lose both heaven and earth.[41]   160

It may be that in these parts,
So laden with learned minds,
Some other perspectives hold;
But in the lands we are from,
This is the way we are taught.[42]   165

39. Sp. "tan fundada en la rapina / y que tanto ha de amargar," literally "so built up on rapine / and that so much bitterness will bring."

40. A literal translation of "como galápago" would read simply "like a turtle"; "galápago" had been a common noun for "turtle" since the fourteenth century. A. G. Solalinde, "Los nombres de animales puros e impuros en las traducciones medievales españolas de la Biblia," pt. 1, *Modern Philology* 27, no. 4 (1930): 83–98; pt. 2, 28, no. 1 (1930): 473–85). Therefore, the mention in the play does not refer specifically to the animals known today as Galapagos turtles, nor to the Galapagos Islands, discovered in 1535 by the bishop of Panama, Tomás de Berlanga. Often referred to as Las encantadas, by the end of the sixteenth century the islands were sometimes referred to as the Galapagos, and they soon appeared on maps as such. Gerard Mercator, for example, depicted the islands in his 1569 projection and labeled them "Galopegos."

41. Line 159 in the original Spanish, "y perderá lo servido," is a partial quote from a popular saying, "sale lo comido por lo servido" (the eaten for the served). This expression is used to describe a business without profit, not worth the effort, where what is eaten (spent) equals what is served (sold). The greedy pursuit of gold in the New World is an even worse type of business because, according to this passage, these rapacious people will lose both the eaten and the served, the gold and the soul; their wealth, because they cannot take it to the afterlife, and their souls, because in their pursuit of gold they become idolaters and commit mortal sins. So in the end they will lose everything: the eaten and the served, the gold and the soul they sold for it.

42. Lines 161–65 are ironic: the chieftain affirms that given the number and grandeur of Spain's men of letters, in Spain ("in these parts") it may well be possible

OTRO   También allá han voceado
que la ley y los profetas
penden en que Dios sea amado,
y el próximo no injuriado;
y estas son las vías rectas.   170

¶ Pues ¿Cómo es esto, Señora?
Y estos apregonan vino
y venden vinagre agora,
despojando cada hora
al indio triste, mezquino.   175
¿Cómo se puede sufrir
entre cristianos tal cosa,
—ni aun bárbaros sé decir—
y la tierra no se abrir
en cosa tan espantosa?   180

ANOTHER   Over there it was also preached
[INDIAN]   That the Law and the prophets hold
                 That God be loved above all,
                 And neighbors never be harmed;
                 That these are the paths to be trod.[43]   170

                 But how is it, O Lady Death,[44]
                 That these people promise you wine
                 And sell you nothing but vinegar,[45]
                 Exploiting hour by hour
                 The poor and suffering Indian?   175
                 How is it possible that Christians
                 Could let such things come to pass,
                 Which even barbarians would scorn,
                 And have the earth not split apart[46]
                 At such a horrible sight?   180

---

to reach some other conclusion (other than the association of greed with the perdition of the soul), but in the Indies ("in the land we are from") this is the lesson that is taught.

43. "Thou shalt love the Lord thy God with all thy heart, and with all thy soul, and with all thy strength, and with all thy mind; and thy neighbour as thyself" (Luke 10:27)

44. The moral character of Death ("La Muerte" is a Spanish feminine noun) is regularly represented as female, though "she" is a skeleton.

45. Sp. "apregonan vino / y venden vinagre." There are multiple layers of irony within these words. First, there is the idea of fraud perpetrated by the people promising salvation (consecrated wine) and delivering bitter suffering (vinegar); evil is thus diabolically disguised as God, which obliterates the evangelical mission. The reference to wine is also (as David Gitlitz rightly notes) an allusion to the Eucharist. "The Political Implications of a Sixteenth-Century Spanish Morality Play," in *Everyman and Company: Essays on the Theme and Structure of the European Moral Play*, ed. Donald Gilman (New York: AMS, 1989), 120. One might add that it is an anastrophe of the transubstantiation, since Christ offered his own blood under the appearance of wine. Jesus not only discloses the true nature of this exterior form, but also delivers much more than what can be seen: salvation. Furthermore, we must remember that during Christ's sacrifice on the cross, he is offered vinegar to drink just before he expires (Luke 23:36)—the final insult to the Son of God (see also Mark 15:36–37).

46. This is a common expression in Spanish for referring to the wrath of God. During the Israelites' journey through the desert, Korah, Dathan, and Abiram and their followers revolted against Moses, who admonished the rebels in vain. God then punished them by making the earth under their tents open apart and swallow them alive along with their possessions: "the ground clave asunder that was under them: And the earth opened her mouth, and swallowed them up, and their houses, and all

CACIQUE   ❡ Imágines de oro y plata
[Fol. 52v] no hacemos; que hemos visto
que esta gente no lo acata;
antes lo roba, arrebata,
aunque fuese el mesmo Cristo.   185
Venimos determinados
dexar los hijos y tierras,
y buscar ya ¡desdichados!
los desiertos apartados
do no nos fatiguen guerras,   190

❡ Donde no haya pestilencia
de oro, ni su maldad
que perturbe la conciencia;
donde justicia y clemencia

CHIEFTAIN[47] Images of gold and silver
[Fol. 52v] We do not worship[48]—a fashion
These people do not respect;
But rather they grab and steal
Even if from Christ Himself.[49]   185
We came to the hard decision
To leave our lands and our offspring
And with broken hearts seek out
Distant, deserted places
Far from the exhaustion of war,[50]   190

Where there exists no epidemic
Of gold, and where its evil
Has no hold upon the conscience,
And where both mercy and justice

---

the men that appertained unto Korah, and all their goods. They, and all that appertained to them, went down alive into the pit, and the earth closed upon them: and they perished from among the congregation. And all Israel that were round about them fled at the cry of them: for they said, Lest the earth swallow us up also. And there came out a fire from the LORD, and consumed the two hundred and fifty men that offered incense" (Numbers 16:31–35).

47. This chieftan may be a different character than the one who introduces the scene.

48. In other words, "We are not idolaters but true Christians." The Indian character declares that the Indians are not making or adoring idols of gold and silver; they are following the biblical mandate and saving themselves from the eternal damnation to be suffered by unrepentant sinners and idolaters: "And the rest of the men which were not killed by these plagues yet repented not of the works of their hands, that they should not worship devils, and idols of gold, and silver, and brass, and stone, and of wood: which neither can see, nor hear, nor walk: Neither repented they of their murders, nor of their sorceries, nor of their fornication, nor of their thefts" (Revelation 9:20). This passage is tailor-made to describe the conquistador's and encomenderos' diabolic worshiping of gold, which, as Las Casas reiterates, is "also idolatry," for it replaces God with gold (Del único modo, 74).

49. Brilliant hyperbole that emphasizes the constant semantic connection—both here and in Las Casas's discourse—between the suffering and sacrifice of Christ and the Indians, and, more importantly, the parallelism between Christ's torturers and murderers and those who afflict the Indians and plunder the New World.

50. According to Las Casas, the Indians "fled to the mountains to get away from such hardened people" (Brevísima, 22). The Indian characters condemn the wars in America in terms similar to the pacifism of Erasmus, an attitude that is also to be found in Scene VI of The Court of Death, which is a moral admonition against the "military state" (fols. 13r–15r; see introduction).

puedan tener libertad.   195
¡Oh, tierra tan malhadada!
quédate allá con tu oro;
déxanos ¡desventurada!
pasar la buena jornada
sin tanta zozobra y lloro.   200

¶ No nos robés el sosiego,
corazón y libertad,
pues están libres de fuego;
y jamás digas te ruego
ser hijos de tu maldad.   205
¿Cómo y por habernos hecho
tan gran merced en mostrarnos
aquel camino derecho
para el cielo, y tal provecho,
se entiende que han de asolarnos?   210

CACIQUE   ¶ Tolomeo que heziste
[OTRO]   tan gran suma y tal conduta

Are allowed their liberty.[51]   195
O unfortunate land
Cling on to your own gold!
O unhappy country! Let us
Live out our days in peace[52]
Without so many sorrows and tears.   200

Do not steal away our quiet,
Neither our hearts nor our freedom,
For these are untouched by fire;[53]
And, I beg you,[54] don't ever say
That we are sons of your evil.   205
What kind of sense does it make,
After they showed us the mercy
Of the path that leads to heaven,
That in exchange for that favor
They'd earned the right to destroy us?   210

CHIEFTAIN[55]   Ptolemy, you who mapped out
                The great number and variety

51. Who are those that should be set free ("puedan tener libertad") thanks to this exile to "deserted places"? In all probability, "justice" and "clemency" from line 194. The chieftain says that in exile they would live in a just and merciful world, with no restraint upon their conscience (that is, they would enjoy freedom of conscience). All of this allows us to venture the hypothesis that this complaint resonates beyond the Indians of the New World and may also allude to the situation of the *conversos* (converted Jews), the New Christians (the descendants of the *conversos*), and even unconverted exiles (see note 102 in introduction).

52. The interpretation of this line is difficult: "pasar la buena jornada" may mean, as suggested by the translation here, "[let us] live out our days in peace," "[let us] spend the day in peace" or "[let us] work the day in peace" ("jornada" could be translated alternatively as "lifetime," "day," or "workday"). On the other hand, "jornada" could refer to a journey (either the entire journey or a day's journey), which is consistent with the preceding talk about an intended exile. So an alternative translation must be kept in mind for this line: "[let us] go our way in peace."

53. In the phrase "libres de fuego," "fuego" (fire) is a metaphor for ire, wrath, rage: "Fire. Understood metaphorically as the ardor ignited by certain passions such as wrath" (RAE, *Autoridades* 1732, 805).

54. Rhetorically addressing the New World, the Indies, full of gold; that is, full of evil.

55. Everything indicates this chieftain may be a different character than the preceding one (see introduction).

de naciones, y escrebiste
di, ¿cómo no nos pusiste
en tu registro y minuta?   215
Antiguos que transtornastes
al mundo, y al retortero
le traxistes y pintastes,
y ¿cómo nos olvidastes,
os pregunto, en el tintero?   220

¶ ¿Cómo no distes noticia
de nuestras tierras? Os pido.
Síguese que la malicia
destos males y cobdicia
más que todos ha sabido.   225
Pues date priesa a criar
mucho oro, ¡oh triste tierra!
porque te quiero avisar

Of nations, and wrote all down,
Why did you fail to include us
In your detailed register?[56]   215
Ancient ones who turned the world
Upside down, and, all distorted,
Sketched it and spelled it out,
Pray tell, how did you miss us,
To leave us behind in the inkwell?   220

How is it that you failed to notice,
I ask you, that our lands were there?
It turns out that the malicious
Cleverness of avarice and evil
Has known better how to find us.[57]   225
Well, O sad land of ours!
Best start making gold in masses,
Because I am here to tell you

56. Claudius Ptolemy, geographer, mathematician, and astronomer from the second century, was born in Ptolemais Hermiou, Egypt, and lived and worked in Alexandria. His *Geography* sums up the work of Eratosthenes, Hipparchus, and Marinus of Tyre, and provides information for drawing maps of the world along with the longitudes and latitudes of nearly eight thousand locations in the three parts of the Ptolemaic world: Europe, Africa, and Asia. "In thirteenth-century Byzantium, Greek scholars equipped the *Geography* with splendid maps. . . . The *Geography* was translated into Latin early in the fifteenth century by the humanist Jacopo d'Angelo. By the middle of the fifteenth century it had become a best seller, as copies newly equipped with colorful maps sailed across the Mediterranean world. . . . The *Geography* reached print in 1475, and many editions, as well as many luxurious manuscripts, attest to its popularity thereafter. . . . It became both a learned authority and a splendid adornment in the libraries of the Renaissance." Anthony Grafton, *New World, Ancient Texts* (Cambridge, Mass.: Harvard University Press, 1992), 49. One famous reader of the *Geography* was Columbus, who was encouraged by Ptolemy's miscalculations of the distance to the East. Ptolemy's *Geography* offered a model of representation of the world open to the inclusion of new data and modifications. Renaissance cartography (particularly atlases) could be characterized as the correction and addition of the maps based on Ptolemy's *Geography*. The chieftain wonders sardonically about the shortcomings of European, classical, medieval, and fifteenth-century knowledge, which overlooked such a vast continent, while greed knew very well how to find it (lines 211–25).

57. The point being that where Ptolemy—as well as all Byzantine and Renaissance geographers—failed, greed and evil triumphed in finding the fourth continent and its riches.

que hay cobdiciosos sin par
que te han de hundir con guerra.   230

¶ Huye pues, entendimiento,
por no contar más maldades
que de aquesta gente siento,
y aquel gran corrompimiento
de leyes y de bondades,   235
aquel jugar al terrero
con los que saben y entienden
que tienen oro y dinero.
¡Oh, mi Dios, tan verdadero,
y en cuántos modos te ofenden!   240

OTRO   ¶ No pensábamos allá
INDIO   que había en el mundo gentes
tan perversos como hay ya;
todos los males de acá
nos fueron y están presentes.   245
¡Cuánto holgamos que prendan,
ahora en tiernas edades,
[Fol. 53r] nuestros hijos, maten, hiendan;
porque no sepan ni aprendan
tantos insultos, maldades!   250

¶ ¿Quién vio nunca en nuestras tierras
arcabuz, lanza ni espada,
ni otras invenciones perras

The plundering armies are near,
Come with their greed to destroy you.   230

Reason, don't linger longer,
Don't make me recount all the evils
I've seen coming from these people
And their terrible corruption
Of virtue and all the laws,   235
Their daring to take for their target[58]
Human beings possessed of reason[59]
To plunder their wealth and gold.
O my one and only God,
In how many ways they offend Thee!   240

ANOTHER We never imagined back home
INDIAN That in all the world there were people
So perverse as these have proven.
All the evils from these parts[60]
Have come to be present with us.   245
How much better it would be
To see our children while young
[Fol. 53r] Slashed, severed, or killed
Than have them take in and learn
So many insults and evils!   250

Whoever saw in our lands
Muskets,[61] lances, or swords,
Or any of those inhuman inventions[62]

58. Sp. "jugar al terrero": target shooting (RAE, *Autoridades* 1739, 259).
59. Literally, "los que saben y entienden" are "those who comprehend and understand." See note to line 140.
60. "These parts" refers to Europe, where the court session is taking place.
61. Sp. "arcabuz": this would be more properly, but more obscurely, translated as "harquebus," a portable firearm that was invented in Spain and was used from the second half of the fifteenth century to the late sixteenth century, when it was replaced by the firearm known as the musket, used from the late sixteenth century through the eighteenth century.
62. The Spanish expression used to talk about those "inhuman inventions" is "invenciones perras," literally "doglike inventions." As in lines 55, 74, and 148, and

de armas para las guerras,
con que sangre es derramada?   255
Nosotros que ciertamente
nos juzgábamos dichosos
por vivir allá en Poniente,
do no hay estruendo de gente,
¿somos los más revoltosos?   260

CACIQUE   ¶ Antes creo, por pensar
que a ninguno mal hacemos,
ni solemos enojar,
todos nos van a tomar
la miseria que tenemos.   265
Vayan a esas amazonas

Of weapons employed in wars
To spill blood upon all sides?   255
We who considered ourselves
Most fortunate to inhabit
The lands of the setting sun,
Far from the noise of crowds—
Are we the most warlike of all?[63]   260

CHIEFTAIN Rather I believe it's because
We do not offer harm to any,
Or give any cause for anger,
That everyone runs to steal
Even the poverty we have.   265
Let them try it with the Amazons,[64]

---

as indicated in the note to line 148, the word "dog"—here as an adjective, "perras"—
functions with a negative semantic charge.

63. Except for a few periods and colons, there is no additional punctuation in
the Spanish original. We prefer to read line 260 as interrogative: "¿somos los más
revoltosos?" ("Are we the most warlike of all?"), given the response of the chieftain
immediately thereafter, "Rather I believe it's because . . . " (261). Line 260 could
alternatively be translated with an exclamation mark, so that it would be understood
ironically.

64. The chieftain invites the conquistadors to try their courage with the legendary Amazons instead of bothering and afflicting peaceful people. The Amazons are
part of the classic and medieval teratologies that informed the ethnographic concep-
tualization of the New World and its inhabitants. According to Herodotus, they were
skillful female warriors and assassins of men who once a year had sexual relationships
and conceived children with the Scythians. Herodotus, *The Histories*, trans. Aubrey
De Sélincourt (London: Penguin, 1996), 249–51. At the end of Columbus's first trip,
the admiral was "informed" about the mythic island of Matinino, "completely popu-
lated by women without men" (*Textos y documentos completos*, 115). Columbus
mentions them often in his diary between January 6 and January 18, 1493. Though
he never found them, he did not dismiss them as imaginary. As he did in the case
of other monsters, he concluded that the Amazons were located farther away, in an
"unknown land" or terra incognita full of gold and cannibals. Those cannibals—like
the Scythians in Herodotus—copulated with the Amazons once a year, forming a sort
of ephemeral American family that distributed the custody of the children from those
unions according to gender: the girls to their mothers and the sons to their fathers
(ibid., 119; Anglería, 1:117). Juan de Grijalva, Francisco de Orellana, and many others
followed rumors and traces of the Amazons in vain. This search, as well as the belief
in their existence, was soon dismissed as futile by historians such as Anglería, Fernán-
dez de Oviedo, and Francisco López de Gómara. But the myth made a long-lasting
impression on the European imagination.

que bien defienden su roca
como varones personas;
y no a unas tristes monas
a quien todo el mundo coca.   270

¶ ¿Qué injuria o qué villanía,
o qué deshonra o despecho,
les habemos hecho hoy día,
porque tal carnicería
hagan en nos, como han hecho?   275
¿Robámosles por ventura
sus campos, sus heredades,
sus mujeres? ¿Qué locura
es ésta, y tal desventura
de tantas enemistades?   280

OTRO   ¶ Dessa que llaman riqueza
INDIO   esa gente tan sedienta
         se cargue, y de su vileza;
         que nuestra naturaleza

Who know how to defend their lands
Like the fiercest of men,
And not like a clutch of monkeys
Any coward could scare away.[65]   270

What harm or what evil turn,
What insult or what dishonor
Are we responsible for,
To account for such a butchery
As these people bring on our heads?   275
Did we by some chance despoil
Their fields, their patrimonies,
Their wives? What madness
Is this, what is the tragic cause
For this hatred without end?[66]   280

ANOTHER   All that they consider riches,
INDIAN   For which they constantly thirst,
             Let them have it, with its evil;
             As for our part, it's our nature

---

65. What is translated here as "to scare away" corresponds to the Spanish "coca," third person singular in the present tense of the archaic verb "cocar," which means to frighten somebody, usually a child, with the "coco," the Spanish version of the bogeyman or a hobgoblin. Covarrubias's dictionary, published only half a century after *The Court of Death*, gives the same definition ("to scare away") with a different etymology: "*cocar*" is "to make *cocos*, as in the sounds that the mother monkey makes to scare kids away to protect herself" (*Tesoro de la lengua castellana o Española*, s.v. "cocar"). Covarrubias's dictionary mentions female monkeys ("monas"), as does the chieftain (269), which should persuade us to accept this zoological onomatopoeia, if not as the origin of the verb "cocar," then definitely as clear evidence of its contextual meaning. There are other possible interpretations worth mentioning: first, the verb "cocar" may be understood as "dar un coco," to smack somebody, since "coca," as a noun, is another "humorous word for head . . . and for the smack a person receives on the head." Joan Corominas, *Diccionario crítico etimológico de la lengua castellana*, 4 vols. (Berna: Editorial Francke, 1954), s.v. "coca." Finally, there may be a transcription error—if "coca" was meant to be "toca" (touch, handle), then the chieftain is saying that the Amazons are not "like a clutch of monkeys / Any coward could handle."

66. In other words, the chieftain is alleging the lack of provocation or the absence of a just cause for war, a topic related to the Valladolid Debate between Las Casas and Ginés de Sepúlveda (see introduction).

con muy poco se contenta.   285
A los que allá van tocados
de aquesa maldita roña,
carga de vasos preciados
do beberán los cuitados
aquel tósigo y ponzoña.   290

¶ Que nosotros no buscamos
más riquezas ni heredades;
con esto nos contentamos,
con saber que sojuzgamos
nuestras proprias voluntades;   295
y ésta tenemos allá
por muy gran filosofía
y cristiana. No sé acá
cómo no se siente ya;
cierto sabello querría.   300

CACIQUE   ¶ ¡Ay! Que no vemos, cuitados,
como andamos con candiles,
que allá somos tan malvados,
que por los nuestros pecados
vienen estos alguaciles.   305
Ni carece de misterio
enviar siempre quien rija

To be contented with little.[67]   285
For those who arrive at our shores
By that damned sickness possessed,
Let them have the precious cups
From which, sad things, they may drink
All the poison and bitterness they wish.   290

As for us, we are not in search
Of riches or great estates;
We are quite happy to know just this:
To know that we are in control
Of our wants and of our will;   295
And over there we consider
This philosophy both grand
And Christian. I don't understand
How it's not seen that way here.
I truly wish that I did.   300

CHIEFTAIN   Oh, we unfortunate ones
Must be just too blind to see[68]
What evildoers we are,
That our dark crimes should bring
These lawmen down on our heads.   305
It is a mystery indeed
To send those with power to rule

---

67. The Indians are, as they said before, considered "simple" (97) because of this indifference toward the value of gold and because they do not appreciate wealth. Again, this simplicity turns out to be virtuous, according to Las Casas, who describes the Indians as "very poor people, who little possess nor *want to possess* temporal goods; and for this they are not arrogant, nor ambitious, nor covetous. . . . Their food is such [so modest] that it does not seem to be more slight nor less 'delicious' nor poor than the food of the saintly [hermit] priests in the desert" (*Brevísima*, 15; emphasis added). See notes to lines 93 and 97.

68. In the original, the chieftain says "como andamos con candiles" (it may be because we walk with candles), which is an ironic commentary on how difficult it is for the Indians (or for anybody) to see that these "lawmen" (the conquistadors) come to the New World because of the sins of the indigenous. Of course, the Indian is saying implicitly "we see clearly; we are not evildoers, and it is not because of our sins— but rather due to their sinful disposition—that the conquistadors come to the New World."

nuestra provincia y imperio,
quien con tanto vituperio
nos gobierne y nos aflija.   310

OTRO   ¶ Pues sólo resta saber
INDIO   si en estas Cortes tan dignas
           se pudiese proveer
           [Fol. 53v] cómo quitar el poder
           destas gentes y rapinas;   315
           y si no hay para qué,
           no nos espere más día;
           mas antes nos da tu fe
           ·llevarnos, y luego ve
           a librar tal tiranía.   320

MUERTE   ¶ ¡Oh cuánta razón tenéis
           de quexaros, mis hermanos,
           dese mal que padecéis,
           porque no lo merecéis,
           especial siendo cristianos.   325
           Mas sabé ques necesario

Over our kingdom and land,
And let them press their will upon us
To our great and grievous harm.[69]   310

ANOTHER   It only remains to be seen
INDIAN   If by this honorable court
A judgment could somehow be found
[Fol. 53v] To wrest away the control
From these human beasts of prey,[70]   315
And if there's no remedy here,
Let us live not one more day,
And rather, Death, if you will,
Better carry us away
And free us from such tyranny.   320

DEATH   Oh, how very right you are,
My brothers, to complain
Of this sorrow you are suffering,
Since you so little deserve it,
Good Christians that you are.   325
But bear in mind that the way

69. The chieftain calls the basis for the colonial presence of these "lawmen" a "mystery." Like Las Casas, he contradicts the colonial argument according to which the conquistador is considered a sort of sword of God's justice to punish the sins of the Indians. An example of this logic is offered by Pedro Cieza de León: "Because of these and other sins that these Indians commit, Divine Providence has permitted that . . . only ten or fifteen Christians united [are able] to attack a thousand, ten thousand of them, and vanquish and subject them; I also believe that this does not come about because of our merits . . . but because God wants to punish them by our hand." Pedro Cieza de León, *La crónica del Perú* (Madrid: Historia 16, 1984), 126. For Francisco Vitoria, "not even by the authority of the Pope can the Christian princes separate the Indians by force from sins against nature, nor [can they] punish them for [those sins]" (*De Indis*, 133). For Las Casas, the Spaniards are not an instrument of God. He contends that in many cases it is, on the contrary, the Indians who have served to punish the sins of the Spaniards.

70. This is the concrete *petitum* by the Indians; they ask the court to rule ("proveer") against the power of the encomenderos. The following lines make a subsidiary petition or demand: if the court cannot "provide" or rule to strip the colonial power from these people ("cómo quitar el poder"), then, in the eventual absence of such a ruling, they ask the courts to provide a merciful death for the plaintiffs themselves: "And if there's no remedy here, / Let us live not one more day" ("y si no hay para qué / no nos espere más día") (316–17).

venga escándalos y guerras,
y tiempo adverso y contrario;
mas ¡ay del triste adversario
por quien vienen en las tierras!   330

¶ Todo lo tened en nada
pues ha placido al Señor
daros en su Iglesia entrada,
y seáis de la manada
de tal rebaño y Pastor;   335
y pues él os libró ya
de otros demonios mayores
que os quieren tragar allá,
creedme que os librará
destos lobos robadores.   340

Is strewn with scandals and wars
And times of travail and trouble.[71]
But woe unto the enemy
By whom the offenses come![72]   330

But all this you must hold as nothing,
Since the good Lord has seen fit
To allow you into his Church
To become part of the flock
Of a Shepherd[73] such as He,   335
And since already He freed you
From great demons over there
That want to swallow you whole,[74]
Believe me when I say He'll save you
From these marauding wolves.[75]   340

71. Death is paraphrasing the Bible to give a theological dimension and a transcendent meaning to colonial injustices: "And ye shall hear of wars and rumours of wars: see that ye be not troubled: for all these things must come to pass, but the end is not yet" (Matthew 24:6). "The Son of man must suffer many things, and be rejected of the elders and chief priests and scribes, and be slain, and be raised the third day" (Luke 9:22), etc. According to Death, suffering is necessary for salvation.

72. Through another biblical paraphrase, Death defers the advent of justice to the afterworld: "Woe unto the world because of offences! for it must needs be that offences come; but woe to that man by whom the offence cometh!" (Matthew 18:7). Death is implicitly stating that God will take care of all of these scandals and wars later, and that the men who carried out such terrible offences will suffer, by the same token, later (see introduction, Section 5).

73. God as a shepherd and the Church as a "flock of God" are common biblical metaphors: "Now the God of peace, that brought again from the dead our Lord Jesus, that great shepherd of the sheep, through the blood of the everlasting covenant" (Hebrews 13:20); "And Jesus, when he came out, saw much people, and was moved with compassion toward them, because they were as sheep not having a shepherd: and he began to teach them many things" (Mark 6:34), etc. The Church will see its mission in the New World through this pastoral metaphor: to take spiritual care of the defenseless flock of the New World.

74. The "greater demons" were the indigenous gods that demanded human sacrifice.

75. In these lines, Death agrees with the plaintiffs and reiterates the Lascasian tropes of the shepherd, the flock, and the voracious wolves. According to Las Casas, the encomenderos and conquistadors were hungry wolves among innocent lambs. In consonance with the metaphor of the pastor/shepherd—which defines the Church and the empire—the Indians are represented by the Dominican friar as "very tame lambs" and "sheep," sacrificed in slaughters (Brevísima, 54–55; see also Del único

¶ Servid a Dios, mis hermanos,
con corazón limpio y puro,
agora que sois cristianos;
y guardaos destos tiranos,
que rondan ya vuestro muro.   345
No creáis cosa que os digan;
catad que son pestilencia
del alma y los que la ligan
y a los tormentos la obligan
si no hallan resistencia.   350

SAN ¶ Hermanos, pues sois del bando
AGUSTÍN de Cristo, os quiero avisar
que ora es día, y vais obrando;
que verná la noche cuando
ninguno podrá ya obrar.   355
Ora que hay tiempo y sazón,
tené al tiempo por la frente;

Serve God well, my brothers,
With a pure and limpid heart,
Now that you've become Christians,
And watch yourselves against tyrants
Who lay siege outside your walls.   345
Believe nothing that they say,
Beware, that they're a pestilence
For the soul, and they would bind it
And force it to eternal torment
Unless some resistance they find.[76]   350

SAINT   Brothers, since you belong
AUGUSTINE   To the hosts of Christ, I advise you
That day's here, the time for working,
That soon the night is coming
When no man can work.[77]   355
Now while the time is in season
Consider what lies ahead[78]

---

modo, 190–95). The biblical echoes, again, are fundamental: the conquistadors and encomenderos had perverted Christ's command to his disciples to go and preach like sheep among wolves (Matthew 10:16), thus, becoming the "false prophets" that the Bible refers to as "ravening wolves" "in sheep's clothing" (Matthew 7:15).

76. See lines 141–50, where the Indians put forth the notion of a rebellion, as well as the footnotes to lines 82 and 145. In contrast, in line 350 the reference to resistance ("resistencia") recommended by Death seems closer to a sort of religious defiance than to a political rebellion against tyrants. It is a revolt in the realm of conscience: "Believe nothing that they say" ("no creais cosa que os digan") (346). In sum, Death recognizes the injustices denounced by the Indian plaintiffs, but the only thing she says in her thirty-line intervention is that injustice is necessary, that the guilty will be judged and punished by God in the afterlife, that the Indians should disregard all these injustices because God will save them (although it will take a while), and that they should resist the pestilent oppressors by not believing what they say. In other words, your argument has merit, but the sentence must wait until Judgment Day. Exactly like the empire itself, Death proves to be a powerless, ineffective, and complicit judge in these matters of colonial tyranny, the exploitation of the Indians and the violence against them. The saints then intervene, rubber-stamping Death's "judgment"; in doing so, they too consent to colonial injustice (see introduction, Section 5).

77. "I must work the works of him that sent me, while it is day: the night cometh, when no man can work" (John 9:4).

78. In the context of the biblical quotation (see preceding note), this line would indicate that Saint Augustine asks the Indians not to look at the present situation and invites them to wait for the future. Therefore, for now, the Indians should work as

ya sabéis su condición,
que es volar, y no es razón
que se os vaya eternamente.   360

SANTO   ¶ La palabra divinal
DOMINGO   oíd siempre, mis amados,
               ques midecina real,
               y veo muy cierta señal
               para ser predestinados.   365

SAN   Porque siempre vais bebiendo
FRANCISCO   de los divinales ríos,
               como yo espero y entiendo:
               sobre todo os encomiendo
               los pobres, hermanos míos.   370

You well know that time's nature
Is to fly, which doesn't mean
Time itself will fly forever.[79] 360

SAINT Listen always, my beloved,
DOMINIC To the word of God Almighty,
The most royal of all *medicines,*[80]
And I would consider it certain
That you are destined for salvation. 365

SAINT Since always you are drinking
FRANCIS From the heavenly fountains,[81]
As I understand and believe,
I recommend to you specially
The care of the poor, my brothers.[82] 370

---

they must, because now is the time to do so ("is time for working")—at least till the night comes; then, no one will work.

79. The condition of time is that of constantly fleeing, according to the classic formula "tempus fugit" and the common saying "time flies" (el tiempo vuela). The saint is recommending patience to the Indians. That patience, of course, translates to the mandate to "keep working."

80. Instead of the standard "medicina," Saint Dominic says "midecina," with a metathesis of the two first vowel sounds (this variant can still be found in rural areas of Spain and Latin America). It must be noted that "medicina" is used elsewhere in the play (line 146). The importance of this linguistic inconsistency is that it confronts us with two signifiers that are semantically and politically antithetical. In other words, the spelling announces and marks a fundamental contradiction. In *The Court of Death,* the indigenous "medicina," like that of the Parthians, is insurrection against tyranny, to make the conquistadors swallow gold (lines 141–50), whereas the "midecina real" of lines 360–65 refers to another kind of remedy: "divine word," patience, and a Christian acceptance of suffering (see introduction, section 5).

81. The saint is drawing on the trope of Christ as a divine fountain, the ultimate and supernatural medicine for all suffering and need: "whosoever drinketh of the water that I shall give him shall never thirst; but the water that I shall give him shall be in him a well of water springing up into everlasting life" (John 4:14). Also: "Jesus stood and cried, saying, if any man thirst, let him come unto me, and drink. He that believeth on me, as the scripture hath said, out of his belly shall flow rivers of living water" (John 7:37–38).

82. An alternative, if different, translation would be "above all I ask you to care / for my poor brothers," meaning Franciscan brothers. But given the Franciscan commitment to the poor, the chosen translation seems more plausible.

¶ ¡Oh Indias, pluguiera a Dios
que vuestra tierra cocida
y oro no diérades vos;
pues por ella hay entre nos
tanta multitud perdida!   375
Porque cuanto allá se afana
con trabajos, con pendencias,
no hay médico que lo sana,
que al fin, fin cuanto se gana
[Fol. 54r] va con muy malas conciencias.   380

SANTO   ¶ ¡Oh cuán pobre fundamento
DOMINGO   armará aquel que hiciere
gran mayorazgo de viento
sobre coluna y asiento
del abismo, cuando muere!   385
¡Dolor de los herederos
que en él han de suceder,
y de sus negros dineros,
que sus pompas y mineros
tan caras les han de ser!   390

¶ Di, India, ¿Por qué mostraste
a Europa esos tus metales
falsos con que la llevaste,
y después nos la enviaste
cargada de tantos males?   395
¿No le bastaban las minas

O Indies, if only the Lord
Had willed that your ore-rich lands
Harbored no gold at all,
Since it has been among us
The cause of so many lost! 375
Because what is won over there
With endless fighting and work,
No doctor can make it safe,
Because in the end the profits
[Fol. 54r] Come with a sickness of conscience. 380

SAINT Oh, what an unsubstantial base
DOMINIC Builds that man who, to make
An inheritance of wind,
Sits on a column that sways
Above the abyss of death! 385
What sorrow of those who come after
To inherit the wealth of their fathers
With the dirty money they left,
And their luxuries and gold mines
How very expensive they'll prove![83] 390

O Indies, why did you show
Europe these treacherous metals
That drew her with their false lure,
Only to send her back home
Loaded with so many evils?[84] 395
Didn't she already have mines,

83. Saint Dominic is alluding to the debate over whether the encomiendas could be legally inherited. Law 30 of the New Laws of 1542 had proscribed this possibility, limiting the power of the encomenderos and producing unrest, even resistance and disobedience among wealthy landowners in the New World. Facing tremendous opposition, Charles V revoked Law 30 by the Royal Provision of October 20, 1545; see Richard Konetzke, ed., *Colección de documentos para la historia de la formación social de Hispanoamérica, 1493–1810*, vol. 1 (Madrid: Consejo Superior de Investigaciones Científicas, 1953), 236–37. Saint Dominic makes explicit reference to the iniquitous triumph of the cause of the heirs and suggests that those who inherit the tainted colonial wealth will pay for it with their souls.
84. Saint Dominic equates evil with gold (the shipment coming from the Indies).

de pecados que tenía
tan profundas y continas,
sino cargarla de espinas
con que mata cada día?   400

¶ ¡Oh India, que diste puertas
a los míseros mortales
para males y reyertas!
¡Indias, que tienes abiertas
las gargantas infernales!   405
¡India abismo de pecados!
¡India rica de maldades!
¡India de desventurados!
¡India que con tus ducados
entraron las torpedades!   410

SATANÁS ¶ ¡Cómo! ¿y piensan de estorbar
que las gentes no pasasen
a las Indias a robar?
y ¿qué negro pie de altar
cogerán si lo pensasen?   415
¿No saben ques el caudal
y la mejor granjería
de la región infernal?
Mas, en fin, el oro es tal,
ques piedra imán que traya.   420

Abundant mines didn't she hold,
Rich enough and deep with sins,[85]
Without you piling on top
The thorns of a daily death?   400

O Indies, who opened the door
To these miserable mortals
Only to bring brawling and sorrow!
Indies, who hold wide open
The very jaws of damnation!   405
Indies, abyss of sinfulness,
Indies, wealthy with evil,
Indies, home for unfortunates!
Indies, that with gold pieces[86]
Paved the pathways of sin![87]   410

SATAN   What? Are they really planning
         To keep the people away
         From plundering the Indies?[88]
         What meager alms[89] instead
         Do they imagine they could get?[90]   415
         Don't they know too well the source
         Of all wealth and prosperous business
         Flows from the pits of Hell?
         For there's no more powerful magnet
         Than gold to drag all in.   420

85. Literally, "the mines / of sin that [Europe] had" ("las minas / de pecados que
tenía").
86. Sp. "ducados" (ducats).
87. The term "torpedades" is translated here as "sin." "Torpedad," in Spanish,
"is the same as knavishness and vileness" (*Tesoro de la lengua castellana o española,*
s.v. "torpedad").
88. Satan is responding to Saint Dominic's discourse against greed and the
hunger for precious metals. Satan embodies here the realistic principle that justifies
primitive colonial accumulation. He is joined by Flesh and World.
89. Sp. "pie de altar": "the alms given to the priests"] (RAE, *Autoridades* 1737,
262).
90. "Do they . . . " referring to the saints. In these lines (411–18), Satan makes
explicit the common interests of the Church and the conquistadors, pointing out that
the Church rewards itself with the very same gold from the Indies that it condemns.

CARNE ¶ Hermano ¿no ves las galas
del mundo fuera de ley?
¡Cuántos palacios y salas!
Y a cada ruin nacen alas
de vestirse como el rey.   425
Pues ¿cómo pueden sufrirse
si no van allá a buscar
para el comer y el vestirse
y si no dexan morirse,
que acá no hay do lo ganar?   430

¶ Las mujeres bastan solas
a echar allá a sus maridos;
que como unas amapolas
andan ya con largas colas
en sus trajes y vestidos.   435
Sustentaldas por ahí
si la India no provee;
que no hay un maravedí,
si no van por ello allí . . .
y allá los quiero, me cree.   440

MUNDO ¶ ¡Gran cosa es la libertad
y estar libres de mujeres
y de hijos, en verdad!

FLESH   Brother,[91] don't you see the luxury
Of a world yours without limits?[92]
Such palaces and such galleries!
And with every pauper dreaming[93]
Of dressing like the king.   425
Why should people deprive themselves
Instead of going there and searching
For something to eat and to wear,
Rather than let themselves die
Looking for means not found here?   430

The wives alone are enough
To speed their husbands abroad,
All dolled up like scarlet poppies,
Dragging behind them the tails
Of their outfits and their dresses.   435
Go and find a way to afford them
Without the Indies footing the bill,
Since there's not a dime[94] to be found
Unless they can dig it up there . . .
And that's just where I want them, you see.[95]   440

WORLD   Liberty is a wondrous thing,
To live unfettered by wives,
To live free of children—that's fine!

91. Addressing Satan.
92. The expression "fuera de Ley" refers to a world without laws or limits, but also to an extraordinary world not comparable with anything else, without law, meaning without known mold or parallel. For this translation we selected the first meaning: a world "without limits."
93. The original Spanish line "Y a cada ruin nacen alas" (literally, "and every plebeian grows wings") quotes a popular saying referring to the lower social classes' bold aspirations of social climbing by virtue of money.
94. Sp. "maravedí."
95. Because of the brusque change in tone, these androcentric lines (430–31) may be an addition to Carvajal's original by Luis Hurtado, or simply a comic or carnivalistic discursive shift congruent with the humorous character of Flesh. In any case, women seem to bear the blame for this modern colonial sin, just as they do for original sin. Their consumerism leads to the damnation of Spain.

La India gran calidad
[Fol. 54v] tiene para los placeres.   445

CARNE   El vivir allá es vivir;
que acá no pueden valerse;
lo que yo te sé decir,
que pocos verás venir
que no mueren por volverse.   450

[Fin de la Escena XIX]

[Fol. 68r, unnumbered] Porque mi sentido
cuadre
con la fe y toda razón
escribo con corazón
de la Iglesia nuestra madre.

*Aquí acaban las Cortes de la Muerte que
compuso Michael de Carvajal y Luis Hurtado de
Toledo. Fueron impresas en la Imperial Ciudad
de Toledo. En casa de Juan Ferrer. Acabáronse el
xv de octubre. Año de MDLVII.*

Indian lands have much to offer[96]
[Fol. 54v] To those looking for some pleasure.   445

FLESH   Life is really life out there,
While here they can hardly make it.
The only thing I can say,
You'll find few back from that place
Who aren't dying to return.   450

[End of Scene XIX]

[Fol. 68r, unnumbered] Because I want for my
thoughts
To fit well with faith and reason,
I write fully from the heart
Of our Holy Mother Church.

*Here ends the Court of Death, written by
Michael de Carvajal and Luis Hurtado de Toledo.
It was printed in the imperial city of Toledo,
in the press of Juan Ferrer. It was finished the
fifteenth of October. Year of MDLVII.*

---

96. During the first half of the sixteenth century, between three and four hundred immigrants a year established themselves in the New World; from 1550 on, that
number increased to two to three thousand (Le Flem, "Los aspectos económicos de la
España moderna," 22–23).

APPENDIX: FACSIMILE OF THE 1557 EDITION

Cortes dela Muerte Alas quales
vienen todos los estados: y por via de representacion: dan
auiso alos biuientes y doctrina alos oyentes. Lleuan
gracioso y delicado estilo. Dirigidas por Luys
Hurtado de Toledo. Al inuictissimo señor
don Phelipe. Rey de España. y ingla
terra. zc. su Señor. y Rey.
Año de. M.D.L.vij.

¶ Luys hurtado de Toledo . Al serenisimo
y muy poderoso señor don Phelipe Rey de España: y Jnglaterra
.xc.su Señor.

Despues de auer dedicado muy alto y muy poderoso señor las cortes de ca
llo amor a vuestra Alteza, halle por mi cuenta quel vulgo publico exami
nado: de agenas causas me auia de juzgar por hõbre vano, mayormēte le
yēdo el espejo ō getileza hospitales ō damas y galanes cõ otras obras ō amor
q a vuestra Alteza offreci. Y para euitar este daño pues la buena opiniõ es jo
ya estimable y mas conel vulgo . Determine tambien para su enmienda y cõ
sideracion de ponelles juntamente otras cortes que hizo la muerte cõ todos
los estados. Con notable llamamiēto eneste año presente En las quales por
apazible estilo y delicadas sentencias cada estado vera lo que dela muerte se
le puede proueer y en las cortes de terminar. Las quales fuere n comēçadas
por Michael de carauajal, natural de Plazencia :y agradado tal estilo yolas
prosegui ya cabe. Ruego al sum mo emperador por cuya voluntad estas cor
tes se hazen cada ora de a vuestra Alteza muchos años de vida contenta y
empleada en su seruicio. Amen.

A B E . MARIA

GRACIA.

PLENA.

A ij

Dela muerte. fo lj.

¶Que más nos vale por año
epicurio y sus consortes
con todo esotro rebaño
q̃ agora hazer tal daño
al infierno en estas cortes
s.agu. Calla calla mal badado
enemigo de bondad
dexa los demonio ayrado
si quiera por tal estado
salir de tal ceguedad

¶Cena.xij. interlo
cutores. Caciq̃ indiomuerte.san
Agustin.s.Fracisco.s.Domingo
satanas. Carne.mundo. Tañen
las trompetas.y entran los
Indios.

caci.¶Los indios ocidentales
y estos caciques venimos
a tus cortes triumphales
a quexarnos delos males
y agrauios que recibimos
Que enel mundo no tenemos
rey ni roque q̃ eche aparte
las rauias que padecemos
y por tanto a ti queremos
muerte dar quexas del arte

¶Pues tu sola ques razon
sabras que siendo paganos
y hijos de perdicion
por sola predicacion
venimos a ser christianos
como aura soy do y visto

seguimos ya la doctrina
y la escuela y disciplina
del maestro jesu christo.

¶Y estamos ya tan vfanos
con la merced singular
de auernos buelto christianos
que alos altos soberanos
no vemos con q̃ pagar
Mas q̃ casos son tan crudos
tu muerte nos da a entender
q̃ quando alos dioses mudos
bestiales falsos y rudos
adorauamos sin ser

¶Ninguno nos perturuaua
de quantos en nuestras tieras
a passado ni passaua
ni mataua ni robaua
ni hazia crudas guerras
y agora que ya cuytados
nos auiamos de ver
vn poco mas regalados
por solo tener los grados
de christiandad en tal ser

¶Parece que desafueros
omicidios fuegos brasas
casos atroces y fieros
por estos negros dineros
nos llueue en nuestras casas
O dios y que aduersidades
son estas no entendeys esto
pagar con mil crueldades
todas las necessidades
del mundo di que es aqsto
b iij

Cortes

CComo estamos obligados
que todo genero humano
enriquezcamos cuytados
y tras esso aperreados
y muertos de agena mano
No nos basta proueer
las miserias de parientes
las de hijos y muger
sino auer de sostener
las de todas essas gentes

CQuiennunca vido al ingles
ni al vngaro ques de porte
ni al bohemio nial frances
ni espanol ni ginoues
de vaxo del otro norte
Por ventura anacabado
todo el mundo despojar
q cosa no aya quedado
pues que con tanto cuydado
nos vayan alla a buscar

Cy como aqllas riquezas
de aquella felice arabia
tarsis saba y sus grandezas
no an hartado las brauezas
de aqsta rauiosa rauia
Los rubies rutilantes
de narsinga tan reales
los safires y diamantes
no anbastado a estos gigantes
sin buscar nuestros metales

Pues mezqnos a do yremos
buyendo del mal gouierno
que mas gente no embiemos

si a nuestra ley nos boluemos
alas penas del infierno
O hambre pestilencial
la de aqueste oro maldito
y desta gente bestial
hazen tamano caudal
de tan maluado apetito

CUna cosa que les damos
de buena gana y en paz
porque alla no lo estimamos
en tanto ni reputamos
por causar males assaz
Que annqlaindia es tenida
por simple cierto no yerra
en despreciarlo y lo oluida
q al fin es tierra cozida
en las venas dela tierra

Que campos no estan regados
con la sangre qa dios clama
de nuestros padres horados
hijos:hermanos:criados
por robar hazienda y fama
q hija muger ni hermana
tenemos queno aya sido
mas q publica mundana
por esta gente tirana
que todo lo a corrompido

CPara sacar los anillos
q dedos no se cortaron
q orejas para carcillos
no rompieron con cuchillos
que braços no destroçaron
que vientres no traspasaron

las espadas con gran lloro
destos males que pensaron
q en los cuerpos sepultaron
nuestros indios su tesoro
   Otro indio.
¶Como: por auer venido
ala vista del señor
ala tarde es permitido
q alos q el vuo querido
roben maten sin temor
¶Pues ellos an predicado
q tanto dio alos postreros
que en su viña an trabajado
como alos que an madrugado
y salieron los primeros

¶Que ley diuina ni humana
permita tales molestias
q a vna gente ques christiana
y q a dios sirue de gana
la carguen como alas bestias
Quien nunca tal vio mortales
me dezid q es compasion
que se siruan delos tales
como de vnos animales
brutos: y sin mas razon

caçi.O partios qn bien curastes
a craso aquel capitan
que por la boca le echastes
tanto oro que matastes
aquella sed y alquitran
Desta mesma medicina
deuieramos cierto vsar
conesta hambre canina
tan fundada en la rapiña

y que tanto a de amargar.

¶Que locuras son aquestas
piensa esta gente enel suelo
q del oro haze fiestas
q a de yr co la carga acuestas
como galapago al cielo
pues tenemos entendido
que si no lo renunciare
q todo es tiempo perdido
y perdera lo seruido
si de tal carga cargare

¶Por ventura como aca
ay tanto y tan gran letrado
otra cosa alcançan ya
pero nosotros alla
ansi nos lo an predicado
otro. tambien alla an bozeado
que la ley y los prophetas
penden que dios sea amado
y el proximo no injuriado
y estas son las vias rectas

¶Pues como es esto señora
y estos apregonan vino
y venden vinagre agora
despojando cada ora
alindio triste mezquino
Como se puede sufrir
entre christianos tal cosa
ni aun barbaros se dezir
y la tierra no se abrir
en cosa tan espantosa

caçi.¶Ymagines de oro y plata
          B iiij

Cortes,

no hazemos que bemos visto
que esta gente no lo acata
antes lo roba arrebata
aun que fuesse el mesmo christo
Tenimos determinados
dexar los hijos y tierras
y buscar ya desdichados
los desiertos apartados
do no nos fatiguen guerras.

¶Donde no aya pestilencia
de oro ni su maldad
q perturbe la conciencia
donde justicia y clemencia
puedan tener libertad.
O tierra tan mal hadada
quedate alla con tu oro
dexanos desuenturada
passar la buena jornada
sin tanta çoçobra y lloro.

¶No nos robes el sossiego
coraçon y libertad
pues estan libres de fuego
y jamas digas te ruego
ser hijos de tu maldad.
Como y por no auernos hecho
tan gran merced en mostrarnos
aquel camino derecho
para el cielo y tal prouecho
se entiende q han de asolarnos.

cac.¶Tholomeo que beziste
tan gran suma y tal conduta
de nasciones y escreuiste
di como no nos pusiste

en tu registro y minuta
antiguos que trastornastes
al mundo y al retortero
le traxistes y pintastes
y como nos oluidastes
os pregunto en el tintero.

¶Como no distes noticia
de nuestras tierras os pido
siguese que la malicia
destos males y cobdicia
mas que todos ha sabido
Pues date priesa a criar
mucho oro o triste tierra
porque te quiero auisar
que ay cobdiciosos sin par
que te han de hundir có guerra

¶Huye pues entendimiento
por no contar mas maldades
q de aquestas gentes siento
y aquel gran corrompimiento
de leyes y de bondades
Aquel jugar al terrero
con los que saben y entienden
q tienen oro y dinero
o mi dios tan verdadero
y en quátos modos te offendé.
¶Otro indio.
¶No pensauamos alla
que auia en el mundo gentes
tan peruersos como ay ya
todos los males de aca
nos fueron y está presentes
Quanto holgamos que prendá
ahora en tiernas hedades

nueſtros hijos maten biendan
porque no ſepan ni aprendan
tantos inſultos maldades.

¶Quien vio nūca en nras trras
arcabuz lança ni eſpada
ni otras inuenciones perras
de armas para las guerras
con que ſangre es derramada.
Noſotros que ciertamente
nos juzgauamos dichoſos
por biuir alla en poniente
do no ay eſtruendo de gente
ſomos los mas reboltoſos.

cac.¶Antes creo por penſar
que a ninguno mal bazemos
ni ſolemos enojar
todos nos van a tomar
la miſeria que tenemos.
Vayan a eſſas amazonas
que defienden bien ſu roca
como varones perſonas
y no a vnas triſtes monas
a quien todo el mundo coca.

¶Que injuria o que villania
o que deſonrra o deſpecho
les auemos becho oy dia
porque tal carniceria
bagan en nos como han becho
Robamos les por ventura
ſus cāpos ſus heredades
ſus mugeres: que locura
es eſta y tal deſuentura
de tantas enemiſtades.

Otro indio
¶Deſſa que llaman riqueza
eſſa gente tan ſedienta
ſe cargue y de ſu vileza
que nueſtra naturaleza
cō muy poco ſe contenta:
Allos que alla vá tocados
de aqueſa maldita roña
carga de paſos preciados
do beueralos cuytados
aquel toſigo y ponçoña.

¶Que noſotros no buſcamos
mas riquezas ni heredades
con eſto nos contentamos
con ſaber que ſojuzgamos
nueſtras proprias voluntades
y eſta tenemos alla
por muy gran pbiloſopbia
y chriſtiana: no ſe aca
como no ſe ſiente ya
cierto ſabello querria.

cac.¶Ay q̄ no vemos cuytados
como andamos con candiles
que alla ſomos tan maluados
que por los nueſtros peccados
vienen eſtos alguaziles.
Mi careſce de myſterio
embiar quien ſiempre rija
nueſtra prouincia y imperio
quien con tanto vituperio
nos gouierne y nos aflixa
Otro indio.
¶Pues ſolo reſta ſaber
ſi en eſtas cortes tan dignas
ſe pudieſſe proueer

como quitar el poder
destas gentes y rapinas
y si no ay para que
no nos espere mas dia
mas antes nos va tu fe
lleuarnos y luego ve
a librar tal tirania.

mue.Có quanta razon teneys
de quexaros mis hermanos
desse mal que padeceys
porq nolo mereceys
especial siendo christianos
Mas sabe ques necessario
venga escandalos y guerras
y tiempo aduerso y contrario
mas ay del triste aduersario
por quien vienen enlas tieras

¶ Todo lo tened en nada
pues a plazido al señor
daros en su yglesia entrada
y seays dela manada
de tal rebaño y pastor
y pues el os libro ya
de otros demonios mayores
que os quieren tragar alla
credme que os librara
destos lobos robadores

Seruid a dios mis hermanos
con coraçon limpio y puro
agora que soys christianos
y guardaos destos tiranos
que rondan ya vuestro muro
no creays cosa que os digan

Cortes,

catad que son pestilencia
del alma y los que la ligan
y alos tormentos la obligan
sino hallan resistencia

f.agu.Dfos pues soys del vádo
de christo os quiero auisar
que ora es dia y vays obrádo
que verna la noche quando
ninguno podra ya obrar:
Ora que ay tiempo y sazon
tene al tiempo por la frente
ya sabeys su condicion
q es bolar y no es razon
q se os vaya eternamente

f.bo.¶ La palabra diuinal
oyd siempre mis amados
ques midecina real
y veo muy cierta señal
para ser predestinados
f.frá.Porq siépre vays beuiédo
delos diuinales rios
como yo espero y entiendo
sobre todo os encomiendo
los pobres hermanos mios

¶ O indias pluguiera a dios
que vuestra tierra cozida
y oro no dierades vos
pues por ella ay entre nos
tanta multitud perdida
Porque quanto alla se afana
contrabajos con pendencias
no ay medico q lo sana
q al fin fin quanto se gana;

Delamuerte   fo. liiij

va con muy malas cōciencias

f.do.C Oquā pobre fundamēto
armara aquel q̃ hiziere
gran mayorazgo de viento
sobre coluna y asiento
del abismo quando muere
Dolor delos crederos
que enel ande suceder
y de sus negros dineros
que sus pompas y mineros
tan caras les ande ser

C Di india porque mostraste
a europa essos tus metales
falsos con que la lleuaste
y despues nos la embiaste
cargada de tantos males
Nole vastauan las minas
de peccados que tenia
tan profundas y continas
sino cargarla de espinas
con que mata cada dia

C O india q̃ diste puertas
alos miseros mortales
para males y rebiertas
indias que tienes abiertas
las gargantas infernales
india abismo de peccados
india rica de maldades
india de desuenturados
india que con tus pucados
entraron las torpedades

fat,C Como y piesan de estoruar

que las gentes no passasen
alas indias a robar
y que negro pie de altar
cojerā si lo pensasen
no saben ques el caudal
y la mejor grageria
dela region infernal
mas en fin el oro es tal
ques piedra y mā q̃ traya

ca.C Hermano no ves las galas
del mundo fuera de ley
quātos palacios y salas
y a cada ruyn nacē alas
de vestirse como el rey
Pues como pueden sufrirse
sino vā alla a buscar
para el comer y el vestirse
y sino verā morirse
q̃ acano ay do lo ganar

C Las mugeres vastā solas
a hechar alla a sus maridos
q̃ como vnas amapolas
andā ya cō grādes colas
en sus trages y vestidos
Sustentaldas por ay
si la india no prouee
q̃ no ay vn marauedi
sino vā por ello alli
y alla los quiero me cree

mū.C Grā cosa es la libertad
y estar libres de mugeres
y de bijos en verdad
la india grā calidad

Coztes,

tiene para los plázeres
car. El viuir alla es viuir
  que aca no pueden valerse
  lo q̃ yo.te se dezir
  que pocos veras venir
  que no mueren poz voluerse

¶ Cena. xx. Tañen
las trópetas y vienen los judios
y mozos. y vn chziftiano poztugues. interlocutozes. don Moy
fen. don fanton. don faron. don
micen judios. muerte. f. agu
ftin. f. jeronimo. fatanas.
  mundo. f. francifco. y a-
    riq̃. y arfaxaz. mozos
poztugues vafco figueyza.

moi. ¶ Tene tene que en faber
  que voy donde efta la muerte
  poz el dio pode y s creer
  q̃ aqui me quiero caer
fátõ. tenti pzimo tenti fuerte
moi. Todos vamos a cuchillo
  fon que ella es muy couarde.
  cierto no me marauillo
  antes tiene vn bomezillo
  tan cruel q̃ dios nos guarde

fara. yo quiero tomár la mano
  y entrar la luego a hablar
moi. no te lo confejo hermano
  el pollo con el milano
  no fe deue de burlar
  el gato con el raton
  el lobo conel cozdero

es ruyn conuerfaciõ
nunca bufq̃s la ocafion
q̃ fiempze fue mal aguero

fara. ¶ No conuiene q̃ tardemos
  ya q̃ q̃ifimos venir
  cumple nos q̃ defpachemos
mi. tomemos huelgo y entremos
  q̃ vna vez fe a de mozir
fara. Demos vn filo pzimero
  rauiofo a nueftras efpadas
  q̃ con mi joyofa efpero
  fino haze lo q̃ quiero
  de acoztalle las pifadãs

mue. Que mãda la gẽte bõzadã
fara. feñoza befar tus pies
moy. no la veys defcuaderuada
  poz el dio q̃ no me agrada
  do a fuego la mala res
  y efta es la q̃ me alauauan
  no la abuzio con tal gefto
  q̃ ya fe me efpeluznauã
  los cauellos y erizauã
  q̃ vifta para de pzefto

fara ¶. Uiuo yo quiẽ me engaño
  tene tene q̃ me cayo
  fare teftamento yo
  questa vez no efcapo no
  de fus manos q̃ defmayo
fátõ· pzimo pzimo q̃ fentifte
  de ver la defnarigada
fara. gua ya s de mi no lo vifte
  ay q̃ a binco me dio trifte
  vuelos papea la embazada

Acuña-Soto, Rodolfo, David W. Stahle, Malcolm K. Cleaveland, and Matthew D. Therrell. "Megadrought and Megadeath in 16th Century Mexico." *Historical Review* 8 (2002): 360–62.

Adorno, Rolena. "Los debates sobre la naturaleza del indio en el siglo XVI." *Revista de estudios hispánicos* 9 (1992): 47–66.

———. *The Polemics of Possession in Spanish American Narrative*. New Haven: Yale University Press, 2007.

Alonso Pedraz, Martín. *Diccionario medieval español: Desde las Glosas emilianenses y silenses (s.X) hasta el siglo XV*. Salamanca: Universidad Pontificia de Salamanca, 1986.

Altman, Ida. "The Revolt of Enriquillo and the Historiography of Early Spanish America." *Americas* 63 (2007): 587–614.

Anglería, Pedro Mártir de. *Décadas del Nuevo Mundo*. 2 vols. Mexico City: J. Porrúa, 1964.

Arias, Santa. *Retórica, historia y polémica: Bartolomé de las Casas y la tradición intelectual renacentista*. Lanham, Md.: University Press of America, 2001.

Baltrusaitis, Jurgis. "Danzas macabras y cadáveres descompuestos." In *La Edad media fantástica*, 2nd ed., 236–49. Madrid: Cátedra, 1987.

Báñez, Domingo. *De Iure et Iustitia Decisiones*. Salamanca: Joannem and Andream Renaut, 1594.

Barrera y Leirado, Cayetano Alberto de la. *Catálogo bibliográfico y biográfico del teatro antiguo español: Desde sus orígenes hasta mediados del Siglo XVIII*. Madrid: M. Rivadeneyra, 1860.

Barthes, Roland. "La mort de l'auteur." In *Le bruissement de la langue*, 61–67. Essais critiques 4. Paris: Seuil, 1984.

Bataillon, Marcel. *Erasmo y España: Estudios sobre la historia espiritual del siglo XVI*. Mexico City: Fondo de Cultura Económica, 1996.

Benjamin, Walter. *Illuminations*. New York: Schocken Books, 1988.

Benzoni, Jerónimo. *La Historia del Mondo Nuovo*. In *América de Bry, 1590–1634*, by Teodoro de Bry, edited by Gereon Sievernich, 150–246. Madrid: Siruela, 1992.

Blanco Sánchez, Antonio. *Entre Fray Luis y Quevedo: En busca de Francisco de la Torre*. Salamanca: Gráficas Cervantes, 1982.

Bry, Teodoro de. *América de Bry*. Edited by Gereon Sievernich. Madrid: Siruela, 1992.

Camões, Luís de. *The Lusíads*. Translated by Landeg White. Oxford: Oxford University Press, 1997.

Cano, Melchor. "Dominio sobre los indios." In Pereña, *Misión de España en América, 1540–1560*, 90–147.

Carranza, Bartolomé de. "¿Por razón de fe puede el Cesar hacer la guerra y retener a los indios del Nuevo Orbe?" In Pereña, *Misión de España en América, 1540–1560*, 38–57.

Carvajal, Michael de. *Cortes de la muerte a las cuales vienen todos los estados: Y por vía de representación dan aviso a los vivientes y doctrina a los oyentes*. Edited by Luis Hurtado de Toledo. Toledo: Juan Ferrer, 1557.

———. "Escena XIX" of *Cortes de la Muerte*. Edited by Carlos Jáuregui. In *Querella de los indios en las "Cortes de la Muerte" (1557) de Michael de Carvajal*, by Carlos Jáuregui, 103–31. Mexico City: Universidad Nacional Autónoma de México, 2002.

———. *Tragedia Josephina*. Edited by Joseph Gillet. Princeton: Princeton University Press; Paris: Les Presses universitaires de France, 1932.

Cassius Dio. *Dio's Roman History*. Vol. 3. Translated by Earnest Cary. Loeb Classical Library 53. Cambridge, Mass.: Harvard University Press, 1914.

Castillo, Susan. *Performing America: Colonial Encounters in New World Writing, 1500–1786*. London: Routledge, 2005.

Cervantes Saavedra, Miguel de. *Don Quijote de La Mancha*. Madrid: Real Academia Española; Asociación de Academias de la Lengua Española; Alfaguara, 2004.

Cieza de León, Pedro. *La crónica del Perú*. Madrid: Historia 16, 1984.

Clark, James Midgley. *The Dance of Death in the Middle Ages and the Renaissance*. Glasgow: Jackson, 1950.

Columbus, Christopher. *Textos y documentos completos: Relaciones de viajes, cartas y memoriales*. Edited by Consuelo Varela. Madrid: Alianza, 1984.

Corominas, Joan. *Diccionario crítico etimológico de la lengua castellana*. 4 vols. Berna: Editorial Francke, 1954.

Cortés, Narciso Alonso. "Miguel de Carvajal." *Hispanic Review* 2 (1933): 141–48.

Covarrubias, Diego de. "Justicia de la guerra contra los indios." In Pereña, *Misión de España en América, 1540–1560*, 184–231.

Covarrubias, Sebastián de. *Tesoro de la lengua castellana o Española*. Barcelona: S.A. Horta, I. E., 1943.

Dança general [de la Muerte]. Manuscrito b.IV.21, Biblioteca del Monasterio del Escorial.

Dante Alighieri. *Purgatorio*. Translated by Jean Hollander and Robert Hollander. New York: Doubleday, 2003.

Derrida, Jacques. *Dissemination*. Translated by Barbara Johnson. Chicago: University of Chicago Press, 1981.

———. *Specters of Marx: The State of the Debt, the Work of Mourning, and the New International*. Translated by Peggy Camuf. New York: Routledge, 1994.

Eichenberg, Fritz. *Dance of Death: A Graphic Commentary on the "Danse Macabre" Through the Centuries*. New York: Abbeville Press, 1983.

Finch, Fe María de Varona. "A Study of *Las Cortes de la Muerte* by Micael de Carvajal and Luis Hurtado de Toledo." M.A. thesis, University of North Carolina at Chapel Hill, 1982.

Foucault, Michel. "Qu'est-ce qu'un auteur?" *Bulletin de la Société Française de Philosophie* 63 (1969): 73–104.

Franchi, Fabio. "Poetiche raguaglio di Parnaso." In *Essequie poetiche overo lamento delle muse italiane in morte del Sig. Lope de Vega, insigne & incomparabile poeta spagnuolo*. Venice: Appresso Ghirardo Imberti, 1636.

García-Bermejo Giner, Miguel M. *Catálogo del teatro español del siglo XVI: Índice de piezas conservadas, perdidas y representadas*. Salamanca: Ediciones Universidad de Salamanca, 1996.

Gillet, Joseph. Introduction to *Tragedia Josephina*, by Michael de Carvajal, edited by Joseph Gillet, xi–lxiv. Princeton: Princeton University Press; Paris: Les Presses universitaires de France, 1932.

Gitlitz, David. "Carvajal's *Cortes de la Muerte:* La actitud cristiano-nueva en *Las Cortes de la Muerte*." *Segismundo* 9 (1974): 141–64.

———. "Conversos and the Fusion of Worlds in Micael de Carvajal's *Tragedia Josephina*." *Hispanic Review* 40 (1972): 260–70.

———. The Political Implications of a Sixteenth-Century Spanish Morality Play." In *Everyman and Company: Essays on the Theme and Structure of the European Moral Play*, edited by Donald Gilman, 111–28. New York: AMS, 1989.

Grafton, Anthony. *New World, Ancient Texts*. Cambridge, Mass.: Harvard University Press, 1992.

Hanke, Lewis. *Aristotle and the American Indians: A Study in Race Prejudice in the Modern World*. London: Hollis and Carter, 1959.

———. "More Heat and Some Light on the Spanish Struggle for Justice in the Conquest of America." *Hispanic American Historical Review* 44 (1964): 293–340.

———. "Pope Paul III and the American Indians." *Harvard Theological Review* 30 (1937): 56–102.

———. *The Spanish Struggle for Justice in the Conquest of America*. Philadelphia: University of Pennsylvania Press, 1949.

Henríquez Ureña, Pedro. *La cultura y las letras coloniales en Santo Domingo*. Buenos Aires: Universidad de Buenos Aires, 1936.

Hermenegildo, Alfredo. "Política, sociedad y teatro religioso del siglo XVI." *Criticón*, nos. 94–95 (2005): 33–47.

Herodotus. *The Histories*. Translated by Aubrey De Sélincourt. London: Penguin, 1996.

Infantes, Víctor. *Las danzas de la Muerte: Génesis y desarrollo de un género medieval (siglos XIII–XVII)*. Salamanca: Ediciones Universidad de Salamanca, 1997.

Invernizzi, Guglielmo, Nicoletta Della Casa, and Maria Canella. *Immagini della danza macabra: Nella cultura occidentale dal Medioevo al Novecento*. Florence: Nodo libri, 1995.

Jáuregui, Carlos. "Apetitos coloniales, salvajes críticos y razón de imperio en las Cortes de la Muerte (1557)." *Bulletin of the Comediantes* 58 (2006): 103–40.

——. *Canibalia*. Havana: Fondo Editorial Casa de las Américas, 2005.

——. *Querella de los indios en las Cortes de la Muerte (1557) de Michael de Carvajal*. Mexico City: Universidad Nacional Autónoma de México, 2002.

Jáuregui, Carlos, and Luis Fernando Restrepo. "Imperial Reason, War Theory, and Human Rights in Las Casas's *Apología* and the Valladolid Debate. In *Approaches to Teaching the Writings of Bartolomé de las Casas*, edited by Santa Arias and Eyda Merediz. Approaches to Teaching World Literature. Forthcoming 2008.

Konetzke, Richard, ed. *Colección de documentos para la historia de la formación social de Hispanoamérica, 1493–1810*. Vol. 1. Madrid: Consejo Superior de Investigaciones Científicas, 1953.

Las Casas, Bartolomé de. *Apologética historia sumaria*. Mexico City: UNAM, 1967.

——. *Brevísima relación de la destruición de las Indias*. Madrid: Tecnos, 1992.

——. "Carta a fray Domingo de Soto." 1549. In *OC*, 13:245–48.

——. "Carta al Consejo de Indias." 1534. In *OC*, 13:81–85.

——. "Carta al maestro fray Bartolomé Carranza." 1555. In *OC*, 13:280–303.

——. "Carta a un personaje de la corte." 1535. In *OC*, 13:87–98.

——. *Conclusiones sumarias sobre el remedio de las Indias*. 1542. In *OC*, 13:119–31.

——. *Del único modo de atraer a todos los pueblos a la verdadera religión*. Translated from Latin by Atenógenes Santamaría. Mexico City: Fondo de Cultura Económica, 1975.

——. *Entre los remedios*. 1552. In *Tratados*, 2:643–849.

——. *Historia de las Indias*. Edited by André Saint-Lu. 3 vols. Caracas: Biblioteca Ayacucho, 1986.

——. "Memorial de Fray Bartolomé de las Casas al Consejo de Indias." In *De regia potestate o derecho de autodeterminación*, edited by Luciano Pereña, App., 282–83. Madrid: Consejo Superior de Investigaciones Científicas, 1969.

——. *Memorial de remedios*. 1542. In *OC*, 13:115–18.

——. *Memorial de remedios para las Indias*. 1516. In *OC*, 13:23–48.

———. *Memorial de remedios para las Indias*. 1518. In *OC*, 13:49–53.

———. *Memorial de remedios para Tierra Firme*. 1518. In *OC*, 13:55–60.

———. "Memorial sumario a Felipe II." 1556. In *OC*, 13:309–17.

———. *Obras completas (OC)*. 14 vols. Madrid: Alianza, 1988–98.

———. "Sobre la destrucción de los indios." Ca. 1546. In *OC*, 13:242–43.

———. *Tratados de Fray Bartolomé de las Casas*. 2 vols. Mexico City: Fondo de Cultura Económica, 1965.

———. "Tratado tercero." In *Tratados*, 1:217–459.

———. *Tratado de las doce dudas*. 1564. In *OC*, 11.2.

Las Casas, Bartolomé de, and Rodrigo de Adrada. "Memorial al emperador." 1543. In Las Casas, *OC*, 13:133–59.

Le Flem, Jean-Paul. "Los aspectos económicos de la España moderna." In *La frustración de un imperio, 1476–1714*, by Manuel Tuñón de Lara, Jean-Paul Le Flem, and Joseph Perez, 11–133. Vol. 5 of *Historia de España*, edited by Manuel Tuñón de Lara. Barcelona: Labor, 1982.

Losada, Ángel, ed. Introduction to *Apología*, by Juan Ginés de Sepúlveda and Bartolomé de las Casas. Madrid: Editora Nacional, 1975.

Mariana, Juan de. *La dignidad real y la educación del rey/De rege et regis institutione*. Madrid: Centro de Estudios Constitucionales, 1981.

Marx, Karl. *Capital: A Critique of Political Economy*. Vol. 1. Harmondsworth: Penguin; London: New Left Review, 1976.

Ortega y Medina, Juan. "El indio absuelto y las Indias condenadas en las *Cortes de la muerte*." *Historia Mexicana* 4 (1954–55): 477–505.

Pacheco, Joaquín Francisco, Francisco de Cárdenas, and Luis Torres de Mendoza, eds. *Colección de documentos inéditos, relativos al descubrimiento, conquista y organización de las antiguas posesiones españolas de América y Oceanía*. Vol. 35. Madrid: Ministerio de ultramar, 1875.

Paredes, Vicente. "Micael de Carvajal, el trágico." *Revista de Extremadura* 1 (1899): 366–72.

Pedro, Valentín. *América en las letras españolas del Siglo de Oro*. Buenos Aires: Editorial sudamericana, 1954.

Peña, Juan de la. "¿Es justa la guerra contra los indios?" In Pereña, *Misión de España en América, 1540–1560*, 268–305.

Pereña, Luciano, ed. *Misión de España en América, 1540–1560*. Madrid: Consejo Superior de Investigaciones Científicas, Instituto "Francisco de Vitoria," 1956.

Quijano, Aníbal. "Colonialidad del poder, cultura y conocimiento en América Latina." *Anuario Mariateguiano* 9 (1997): 113–21.

Real Academia de la Lengua (RAE). *Diccionario de la lengua castellana*. [*Autoridades*.] Madrid: F. del Hierro, 1726–37.

———. *Diccionario de la lengua castellana*. Madrid: Joaquín Ibarra, 1780.

Rodríguez-Moñino, Antonio. "El poeta Luis Hurtado de Toledo." In *Las Cortes de la Muerte*, by Luis Hurtado de Toledo and Michael Carvajal, 9–34. Valencia: Librería Bonaire, 1964.

Rodríguez-Puertolas, Julio. "Las Cortes de la Muerte, obra erasmista." In *Homenaje a William L. Fichter: Estudios sobre teatro antiguo hispánico y otros ensayos,* edited by A. David A. Kossoff and José Amor y Vázquez, 647–58. Madrid: Castalia, 1971.

Rubiés, Joan Pau. *Travel and Ethnology in the Renaissance: South India Through European Eyes, 1250–1625.* Cambridge: Cambridge University Press, 2000.

Ruiz Ramón, Francisco. *América en el teatro clásico español: Estudio y textos.* Pamplona: Ediciones Universidad de Navarra, 1993.

Sánchez Arjona, José. *Noticias referentes a los anales del teatro en Sevilla desde Lope de Rueda hasta fines del siglo XVII.* Seville: E. Rasco, 1898.

Saugnieux, Joël, ed. *Les danses macabres de France et d'Espagne et leurs prolongements littéraires.* Lyon: E. Vitte, 1972.

Sepúlveda, Juan Ginés de. *Demócrates Segundo o de las justas causas de la guerra contra los indios.* Madrid: Instituto Francisco Vitoria, 1984.

Sepúlveda Juan Ginés de, and Bartolomé de las Casas. *Apología.* Edited by Ángel Losada. Madrid: Editora Nacional, 1975.

Shoemaker, William. *The Multiple Stage in Spain During the Fifteenth and Sixteenth Centuries.* Princeton: Princeton University Press, 1935.

Suárez, Francisco. *Defensa de la fe católica y apostólica contra los errores del anglicanismo [Defensio fidei Catholicae et apostolicae aduersus Anglicanae sectae errores].* Edited by José Ramón Eguillor Muniozguren. 4 vols. Madrid: Instituto de Estudios Políticos, 1970–71.

Thomas Aquinas. *Summa theologiae.* Cambridge: Blackfriars; New York: McGraw-Hill, 1964.

Varela, Consuelo. "Las Cortes de la Muerte, ¿primera representación del indígena americano en el teatro español?" In *Humanismo y tradición clásica en España y América II,* edited by Jesús María Nieto Ibáñez, 333–49. León, Spain: Universidad de León, Secretariado de Publicaciones, 2004.

Vegue y Goldoni, Ángel. "Apuntaciones para la biografía de Luis Hurtado de Toledo." In *Temas de arte y de literatura.* Madrid: Imprenta Iris, 1928.

Vitoria, Francisco de. *De Indis.* 1539. In *Doctrina sobre los indios,* edited and translated by Ramón Hernández Martín, 103–32. Salamanca: Editorial San Esteban, 1992.

———. *De temperantia.* 1537. In *Escritos políticos,* edited by Luciano Pereña. Buenos Aires: Ediciones Depalma, 1967.

Whyte, Florence. *The Dance of Death in Spain and Catalonia.* Baltimore: Waverly Press, 1931.

Zavala, Silvio. "The Evolving Labor System." In *Indian Labor in the Spanish Indies,* edited by John Francis Bannon, 76–81. Boston: Heath, 1966.

ABOUT THE AUTHORS

CARLOS A. JÁUREGUI. Associate Professor of Latin American Literature and Anthropology at Vanderbilt University and Associate Scholar in the Center for Latin American Studies at the University of Pittsburgh. His book *Canibalia* (Fondo Editorial Casa de las Americás, 2005; 2nd ed., Vervuert, 2008), winner of the 2005 Casa de las Américas Award, focuses on the historical redefinition and ideological values of cannibalism as a shifting cultural metaphor in constructing and contesting Latin American identities throughout various stages of its cultural history. Other publications include *Querella de los indios en las "Cortes de la Muerte" (1557) de Michael de Carvajal* (Universidad Nacional Autónoma de México, 2002); *Heterotropías: narrativas de identidad y alteridad latinoamericana* (coedited with Juan P. Davobe; Instituto Internacional de Literatura Iberoamericana, 2003); and *Of Rage and Redemption: The Art of Oswaldo Guayasamín* (coedited with Joseph Mella and Edward Fischer; Vanderbilt University Press, 2008). His articles have appeared in journals such as *Colonial Latin American Review, Revista Iberoamericana, Revista de crítica literaria latinoamericana, Hispanic Issues, Enunciación, Humboldt* (Goethe Institut), *Revista, Casa Silva, Actual,* and *Revista de Estudios Colombianos.*

MARK SMITH-SOTO. Professor of Romance Languages and Director of the Center for Creative Writing in the Arts at the University of North Carolina at Greensboro, and editor of *International Poetry Review*. He is a 2005 winner of a National Endowment for the Arts fellowship in creative writing, and his poetry has appeared in *Nimrod, Carolina Quarterly, The Sun, Poetry East, Quarterly West, Americas Review, Callaloo, Literary Review, Kenyon Review,* and various other literary magazines. His poetry chapbook *Green Mango Collage* won the North Carolina Writers' Network Year 2000 Persephone Competition. Another short collection, *Shafts,* won the North Carolina Writers' Network's 2001 Randall Jarrell–Harperprints Poetry Competition. He has published two books of poetry, *Our Lives Are Rivers* (University Press of Florida, 2003) and *Any Second Now* (Main Street Rag, 2006).

INDEX

latin american originals

Series Editor | Matthew Restall

This series features primary source texts on colonial and nineteenth-century Latin America, translated into English, in slim, accessible, affordable editions that also make scholarly contributions. Most of these sources are being published in English for the first time, and represent an alternative to the traditional texts on early Latin America. The initial focus is on the conquest period in sixteenth-century Spanish America, but subsequent volumes include Brazil, as well as later centuries. The series features archival documents and printed sources originally in Spanish, Portuguese, Latin, and various Native American languages. The contributing authors are historians, anthropologists, art historians, and scholars of literature.

Matthew Restall is Professor of Latin American History and Anthropology, and Director of Latin American Studies, at the Pennsylvania State University. He is co-editor of *Ethnohistory* journal. J. Michael Francis is Associate Professor of Latin American History at the University of North Florida.

Associate Series Editor | J. Michael Francis

Board of Editorial Consultants

Noble David Cook | Edward F. Fischer | Susan Kellogg
Elizabeth W. Kiddy | Kris E. Lane | Alida C. Metcalf
Susan Schroeder | John F. Schwaller | Ben Vinson III

Titles in print

Invading Colombia: Spanish Accounts of the
Gonzalo Jiménez de Quesada Expedition of Conquest (LAO 1)
J. Michael Francis

Invading Guatemala: Spanish, Nahua,
and Maya Accounts of the Conquest Wars (LAO 2)
Matthew Restall and Florine G. L. Asselbergs

The Conquest on Trial: Carvajal's Complaint of the
Indians in the Court of Death (LAO 3)
Carlos A. Jáuregui